The
Eldest Child

The
Eldest Child

The lonely life of daddy's girl

PENELOPE VAUGHAN

THE CHOIR PRESS

First published in the United Kingdom in 2022 by
The Choir Press

ISBN 978-1-78963-282-8

Prologue

The man stood by the grave of his daughter, his emotions held in check by a combination of his strict upbringing (where emotions were frowned upon) and several large whiskies (an addiction of nearly forty years).

The pastor's voice droned on in the background on this beautiful July day, tainted with tragedy and so much sadness at the pointless death of one so young. As the final Amens were uttered, the man threw twelve red roses into the grave, each thudding eerily and with a resounding finality onto the coffin of his favourite child.

There would be no wake, no happy memories shared, no reassuring hugs or comfort. Nothing that bonded a normal family.

The man just wanted oblivion, as he had sought so much in the past, but particularly on this day.

So he left his two younger children to cope with their grief and shut the door on the last thirty-five years, from when his beautiful wife had first held his eldest daughter in her arms.

Chapter One

The man had grown up as the elder of two children. He was born on his mother's birthday and named John. At some point during his childhood, his mother had told him that he was the worst birthday present she had ever had.

The family lived in the pretty seaside resort of Worthing in West Sussex, in a bungalow that was quite cramped. The Father ran the local greengrocers but unfortunately he was drinking most of the profits. After putting up with her husband's volatile behaviour for several years, his mother reached breaking point and gave him his marching orders.

Raising her small family single-handedly made his mother mirthless and bitter and John grew up in an affectionless home, where children were expected to be 'seen but not heard'.

John was highly intelligent and very studious. He excelled at school and was a year ahead of his peers. His love of books was a source of solace that would stay with him throughout his life.

His mother never praised her children, particularly John, but criticism was doled out on a regular basis, along with undeserved thrashings, which she relished.

Then in 1939 World War Two broke out, and so began six years of great uncertainty.

John and his sister weren't sent away as evacuees as their hometown was deemed to be relatively safe. John would just bury his head in his books and try to avoid his mother's wrath, not always successfully. He would sit and daydream of a life far away from her and he knew that getting a good education was part of the solution.

The war ended six years later and John, by then aged thirteen, finished his education but deferred going to university as he had decided to do his two years of national service, which took him to Egypt (and away from his mother).

On his return to England, he decided against going to university and set about getting himself a job and some digs. He couldn't bear living under the same roof as his mother and she was glad to see the back of him.

He had acquired a reasonable social status since his return from overseas and was attending a few lavish functions, but his easy debonair manner masked a rather shy man who used alcohol as a crutch.

And so began his toxic relationship with alcohol. It would ruin any chance of him sorting out the numerous emotional issues instilled in him from an early age. Whenever a difficult feeling reared its ugly head, instead of addressing it, he would just stare at it through the bottom of a large whisky glass until the persistent pain of being an unloved and fatherless child was eradicated from his thoughts.

The apple certainly hadn't fallen far from the tree.

He was extremely interested in politics and as a staunch conservative, he 'rejoiced greatly' at Churchill's re-election in 1951, although he was still too young to vote.

By his early twenties John had grown into a good-looking man of medium height and slight build, with a mop of wavy black hair and dark brown eyes filled with sadness. His Spanish good looks and clipped upper crust English accent proved to be a winning combination with the ladies, and he was making the most of it.

He became involved with the local amateur dramatic society and with a little 'Dutch courage' became another budding 'Richard Burton'. As he started to land himself major roles in some classic plays he would break many a leading lady's heart, but he had yet to meet his 'Elizabeth Taylor'.

He found gainful employment (for a while) as a driving instructor for the British School of Motoring, but patience wasn't really his strong point and his 'Basil Fawlty' approach to teaching ruffled a few feathers. He decided to quit while he was ahead and started looking for something more suited to his temperament.

The prospect of running his own business appealed greatly to the man, who really was a loner at heart. However, for the time being he took up an administrative post at a car dealers to tide him over. He also took up boxing and was a keen and fairly proficient tennis player.

He would have loved for acting to be his profession, but he knew in his heart that he had to find something with more stability to keep a roof over his head and food on the table. It would have to remain a much-loved hobby.

John's life was pretty full, and for the first time, it was quite enjoyable too.

Chapter Two

———

Elizabeth surveyed the entrance to the magnificent eighteenth-century chateau with a sense of foreboding.

Her taxi had disappeared back along the long avenue that had brought her to this little village north of Paris, and so she had no option but to make her way up the front steps that led to a rather imposing front door.

She rang the bell and was quickly greeted by a member of staff, who ushered her through the doorway. The glorious entrance hall was adorned with sumptuous chandeliers that shimmered in the sunlight that streamed through the stained-glass windows.

She was guided up the grand staircase to her rooms, which were spacious and had lovely views of the gardens. She lay on the bed hugging her bump. It had brought her so much shame, and it had brought her here, banished to this home for unmarried mothers 'in disgrace'.

She had fallen madly in love with Guy, a Belgian RAF pilot. She wondered whether he had guessed what had happened or whether he was still blissfully unaware of her condition. In the 1950s women were seen as 'ruined' if they fell pregnant out of wedlock, and the solution was seen as forcing them to give up their babies for adoption. To add to the heartbreak, the women had to nurse their child for two to three weeks before the baby was wrenched away from them in the most callous fashion and given to the adoptive parents. The women were then supposed to resume the life that they had led before 'the little mishap' and the whole sad chapter was never mentioned again.

The time came one bleak late-winter morning, and after many hours Elizabeth – frightened and alone apart from the nursing staff – gave birth to a beautiful healthy baby boy. She named him Richard.

When the nurses placed her baby in her arms, she felt a love greater than anything she had ever known before, surpassing even her feelings for Guy. She felt as though her heart would burst as she looked into his little face and all she could see was his father, for in her eyes he was his double. Every time she nursed him their bond strengthened, and she would look down at his innocent face and despair inwardly at the inevitable outcome of giving birth to an illegitimate child.

The corridors echoed with a combination of new-born babies crying and the harrowing, inconsolable sobbing of the mothers when they had their children taken from them.

The day that they took Richard from her, they also took part of her soul. It broke her heart into a thousand pieces, never to be made whole again. She sobbed and pleaded and was at the point of collapse as the nurses took Richard out of her arms, and she raced to the windows just in time to see a car disappearing down the long avenue with her baby and his adoptive parents inside.

Bereft, Elizabeth cried herself to sleep at night, consumed with despair and an inconsolable longing.

For her entire life she would grieve for her little boy who was 'stolen' from her, and her heart weighed heavily with an immeasurable sorrow.

She left the chateau a few days later a very different girl to when she'd arrived.

On her return to England, her extremely religious parents made no mention of her 'little problem', and she had very few people to confide in. She felt very much alone, and her relationship with her parents suffered as a result.

To have to keep such a secret was emotionally crippling and very unhealthy. It was only in the final five years of her life that her dark but oh-so-precious secret would be revealed.

***

Elizabeth threw herself into her great passion, which was music. She would travel weekly to her aunt's apartment in Belgravia, where she studied for all her piano grades, and the two of them would make a day of it.

Aunt Irene was diminutive in stature and so incredibly pretty that she looked like a little china doll. She was a famous pianist and had continued to give recitals during the war. Elizabeth adored her and was one of a very few select students that her aunt taught in between recitals.

Irene's apartment was small but palatial, impeccably decorated and housed her most treasured possession, her Bluthner baby grand piano. Elizabeth would immerse herself in her music and for a short time she could put her sadness to the back of her mind and lose herself in 'the classics'. Her aunt knew that Elizabeth was heartbroken, but she never spoke about it. She gave her support and solace in the only way she knew how and when they had finished playing, they would sit outside in the beautiful little garden watching the night sky while enjoying a glass or two of wine.

Elizabeth was still living with her parents in Reading, and she worked as a buyer for Marks & Spencer. This involved quite a lot of travelling, which kept her busy and gave her a decent income. Among her many talents, Elizabeth was a wonderful ballroom dancer. She had entered and won several competitions with her father, Ben, as her dance partner. Her mother, Gwen, was quite disapproving of her 'showy' daughter and kept Elizabeth very much at arm's length (as she did her husband).

Elizabeth was an only child. Gwen loved her husband dearly but was a God-fearing woman and had done her duty as a wife – by consummating the marriage and having a child. Thereafter she insisted on single beds, and her armoury of flannelette nightdresses was enough to dampen the ardour of any man. Her husband, realising sex was such an awful ordeal for his beloved wife, had taken the hint and seemed content enough with their otherwise affectionate and affable marriage.

Elizabeth started to give private piano lessons from her parents' home two or three evenings a week, and Ben became concerned as to whether his beautiful but very headstrong daughter would ever fly the nest and find herself a husband and finally settle down. He loved her dearly but was only too aware that under that well-constructed façade of confident career woman lay a very fragile and broken little girl.

Ben was the son of a Welsh Baptist minister, and his family spent their Sundays in church. He was a wealthy businessman and very well-known and liked through his connections with the church and his work. He also ran and conducted the church choir, and Gwen sang top soprano, while Elizabeth would either sing or play the organ, or both.

Ben saw an upcoming dinner and dance as an opportunity to get his daughter socialising again. He knew Elizabeth was still reeling from her love affair with Guy and since her return from France, men had been completely off the menu.

He eventually cajoled Elizabeth into being his plus-one (as his wife wasn't keen on these 'dos' and was quite happy to stay at home and enjoy an evening of solitude listening to the radio and doing some knitting).

Elizabeth bought a striking netted ballgown and matching black shoes for the occasion and left her thick, wavy, dark brown shoulder-length hair loose. She wore simple jewellery: a pair of diamante earrings and matching necklace. She surveyed her reflection in the full-length mirror and added a bit of lipstick and a dab of Chanel No. 5 and grabbed a shawl.

As she descended the stairs she could see her father impatiently chain-smoking, but when he saw her, she was greeted by his lovely smile that made his eyes twinkle. He told her that she looked enchanting.

A brief chauffeur-driven journey later, Elizabeth and Ben entered the building. All eyes were on this astonishingly striking young woman and her rather dashing and extremely proud father. They were shown to their table and menus were brought to them. The band struck up and the evening had begun.

After a couple of glasses of wine, Elizabeth started to unwind a little and even danced a couple of times with her father.

Several young men asked her to dance, most of whom she declined, but she couldn't help noticing a rather good-looking dark-haired man, with the most soulful eyes, sitting close by who couldn't take his eyes off her. As the evening was drawing to a close, the man had finally consumed enough Dutch courage to stumble over to her table to ask for a dance. She realised he was a little the worse for wear, but there was something about him, so she accepted. Although his dancing was truly atrocious, the moment he touched her, she knew. He was the one. And he had just met his Elizabeth Taylor.

Chapter Three

Elizabeth was feeling a little nervous as she went through her extensive wardrobe for about the fourth time. John had telephoned (as promised) and was taking her to a club that night.

She eventually decided on a green taffeta gown and shawl, with diamond and emerald drop earrings to match. As always she left her wavy hair down, and it loosely caressed her bare shoulders. At 5 foot 1 and with her slender figure, she was most definitely a head-turner.

At eight o'clock the doorbell chimed, and her stomach did a double somersault. She tried to compose herself, but she felt like a teenager again. She could hear her father making small talk with her date and thought that she had better make an appearance in case he changed his mind and did a runner. She made her way down the long staircase into the hall and entered the drawing room, where the two men were sitting politely sipping sherry. Both men rose as she entered the room, her father telling her she looked lovely, and John muttering something similar.

Gwen had made herself scarce and was pottering around in the kitchen listening to Handel's *Messiah*, happily joining in with 'And He Shall Purify'.

Elizabeth shouted goodbye to her mother and kissed her father on the cheek.

They'd decided on a jazz club, and the chauffer drove towards the town centre while John and Elizabeth sat in the back chatting nervously.

Once they'd been shown their table, John made a beeline for the bar. After the pair of them had had a couple of drinks they began to relax and enjoy each other's company.

Elizabeth was nearly seven years older than John, but this didn't bother him; in fact, he was still pinching himself in case this was all a dream. He thought she was an absolute stunner.

He made a couple of attempts to dance with her, mainly to fend off other men, who were breaking their necks in an attempt to catch her eye. John wasn't going to take any chances with this girl. Not only was she good-looking, but she was also talented, intelligent, wealthy – and she quite liked a drink. What more could a man ask for?

Elizabeth was having similar thoughts. It was a long time since she had been out with anyone. John was definitely her type and there was a very strong physical attraction between them.

The evening ended with a passionate kiss and John promised to call her the next day to arrange another date.

It's fair to say that they were both smitten. Love was most definitely in the air.

***

Over the following weeks the whirlwind romance went from strength to strength. They only had eyes for each other and spent as much time as they could together.

They managed to resist temptation for nearly three months, but finally they spent a weekend at a friend's apartment. After two days of exhilarating sex, Elizabeth was glowing, and John was quite exhausted.

Elizabeth was hoping that John would hurry up and pop the very important question – with no foolproof form of contraception at their disposal, she feared she would become pregnant again. Marriage was what they both wanted, and so in due course, and with a certain amount of trepidation, John arranged to meet with Ben to formally ask for his daughter's hand in marriage. Ben was delighted, and once that ordeal was over with, John left Elizabeth and her parents to organise 'the wedding of the year'.

They decided on 21st July, hoping that the British weather would be kind to them. The service was to be at Caversham Baptist Church, followed by a reception at the local hotel. It would be quite a grand event, given Ben's position in the community.

Invitations were sent. Elizabeth found a dressmaker who designed a beautiful full-length, long-sleeved gown with a lace bodice and a full-length double veil with a mother of pearl coronet. The dress was cinched in to show off Elizabeth's tiny waist. The result was understated, demure, classy and elegant, and Elizabeth was delighted with it.

The men were to wear full morning suits with top

hats. The ladies were busily shopping for their outfits, which of course included the hats that were the height of fashion, the pillbox and the teardrop.

John's sister had agreed to be a bridesmaid and had a pretty three-quarter-length dress and flowers in her hair.

They'd booked a harpist to play during the signing of the register. The cake was ordered along with the flowers and the church was filled with beautiful colours and fragrances. Everything was set for a fairy-tale wedding.

***

The morning of the 21st July dawned. John had the hangover from hell (following his stag night) and Elizabeth was very excitable and somewhat nervous preparing for her big day.

At 12:45 p.m. John was waiting in his place in the church, with his best man by his side (equally the worse for wear from the previous night's overindulgences). They had both had to have several 'hairs of the dog' to steady themselves for the day ahead.

The church was filled with people chatting and the organist playing the usual wedding repertoire while waiting for his cue for when the bride arrived.

At 1 p.m. precisely Elizabeth and her father entered the church to the sound of Mendelssohn's 'Wedding March'. The guests rose as the pair made their way down the aisle, slowly and in perfect unison, acknowledging friends on either side as they went, with a smile and a nod, before reaching the altar.

Ben then handed his most precious possession, his daughter, over to his future son-in-law, and the ceremony began.

The responses by the couple were beautifully prepared and delivered, no one forgot the rings, the soloist sang like an angel and by the end of the service, the guests were all dabbing their eyes with rather expensive handkerchiefs (and the odd serviette).

After the final 'I do's, the couple kissed, and Elizabeth and John floated out of the church on cloud nine.

The photographer was eagerly waiting and after a twenty-minute photoshoot, the couple sped off to the hotel for the reception for more photographers, food, speeches, and quite a lot of alcohol.

The day was going perfectly, just as Elizabeth had hoped. She went to get changed into her going away outfit and grabbed her cases quickly as they were set to honeymoon in Ben's holiday home on the Isle of Wight.

As they drove away, they were waved off by their guests, who formed a sea of smiling faces outside the hotel. They arrived at the ferry just in time.

The forty-five minute crossing was relatively calm but seemed like an eternity to Elizabeth and John, who couldn't wait to rip each other's clothes off. Had there been somewhere on board with enough privacy, they would have risked a quickie, but they had to keep up a façade of some respectability until they reached their holiday home in Ryde.

On arrival John clumsily gathered up his tiny bride in his arms and carried her over the threshold, collapsing in a heap on the nearest bed. Ignoring their surroundings, and with only one thing on their minds, the couple rapidly discarded their clothes and enjoyed each other with an insatiable appetite.

It's fair to say that they didn't really see much of their honeymoon destination. They did emerge from their bedroom a couple of times to restock on food, cigarettes and alcohol and even took a romantic moonlight walk by the sea.

In those five days they were blissfully happy and felt that their union was perfect and that together they could achieve anything and everything they'd ever dreamt of.

They knew that they had a lot of work to do on their return to the mainland and were enjoying every second of being 'young, free and totally irresponsible' while they still could.

They didn't want anything to burst that bubble, but on the last night of passionate lovemaking they knew that once they boarded the ferry back to Portsmouth, they would have to come back down to earth with a bump.

The first job would be finding themselves somewhere to live. Elizabeth had been sent to Northamptonshire with her work with Marks & Spencer and Ben had agreed to form a limited insurance company with his son-in-law and be a sleeping partner.

On returning to Caversham, they spent the weekend

at Elizabeth's parents' house and were informed by Ben that he had rented them a two-bedroom flat in Northampton for a year, just to get them started.

Elizabeth was overjoyed and John muttered something about how of course they would repay his great kindness as soon as the business took off.

The following week there was a lot of toing and froing to the new abode with furnishings and knick-knacks. Ben had also bought them a second-hand car as a wedding present. Within a fortnight they were set up in Northampton, approximately seventy miles from Reading.

***

After their first year of married life Elizabeth decided to leave her job at Marks & Spencer and work as a professional musician full time.

John worked from home with his insurance business and was starting to do some networking at the nineteenth hole of the golf club that he had joined.

Elizabeth made enquiries at several schools and a couple of churches and managed to land three music teaching jobs at private schools as well as becoming the organist every other Sunday at a nearby village church. Elizabeth was never slow off the mark and was a very high achiever, so word spread quickly about this new musician in town, and soon her telephone was ringing off the hook.

The little village where she played the organ was

quite quaint and so, again with Ben's help, the couple bought a sweet little cottage there. It was big enough to house an upright piano and had lovely gardens so that the couple could at last have pets. Elizabeth started a local choir. They had weekly choir practice in the cottage's very small dining room while John made his excuses and disappeared to the village pub.

Within three months of moving to 'Adastra', Elizabeth was delighted to discover that she was pregnant. She continued working right up until the last moment and on 20th March 1961 gave birth to a baby girl.

After quite a long labour, John was called into the delivery room to hold his eldest child for the first time. He was overcome with emotion. To think that he had been a part of producing something so perfect was amazing. He swore that he would love and protect this little girl for as long as he had breath in his body.

Jane had inherited her mother's beautiful eyes, and her fine wavy light brown hair came courtesy of her Welsh grandfather's gene. Weighing in at 7 lbs 5 oz, she was very healthy and proving to be a bright, pretty and contented baby.

Over the following two years Elizabeth managed to juggle raising her beautiful daughter along with running the local choir, doing some private piano tuition and still managing her stint as the church organist once a fortnight.

John's insurance company was ticking over, despite him spending rather longer at the nineteenth hole of his club than was advisable when starting out in business.

They had found a reliable babysitter, which enabled the gregarious couple to accept numerous invitations from their new neighbours to dinner parties and drinks at the local pub.

When Elizabeth and John were courting they both drank quite a lot. Since her pregnancy and Jane's birth, Elizabeth had cut down, but John seemed to be drinking more. John's personality changed quite dramatically when he had had too much alcohol, Elizabeth noticed. It brought out a vicious streak in him that quite disturbed her. He became derisory and at times downright cruel. She hoped she would never become the object of his ridicule for she was far too fragile to be on the receiving end of such callousness.

Jane continued to be the most important thing in both her parents' lives and watching her thrive and grow brought them great joy. She was a child who loved to learn and longed to please. Elizabeth and John were both high achievers, so their precious daughter had no other option than to be perfect. From an early age she learnt exactly what kind of behaviour could turn her father's frown into a smile and get him to soften his sometimes stern exterior.

To the outside world this young couple had everything. A home of their own, careers and a lovely little girl. It all appeared idyllic.

When Jane was approaching her third birthday, Elizabeth realised she was expecting again. They hadn't really planned it, but Elizabeth was thrilled. Jane was used to being an only child, but as preparations were being made for her new brother or sister's arrival, she didn't seem too put out.

Again, Elizabeth continued working up until the last couple of months, but John was spending more of his time at the pub, leaving her increasingly dependent on the babysitter.

When she was eight months pregnant and during a rather warm late spring bank holiday weekend, things took a disturbing turn for the worse: John did a disappearing act. He had offered to go to the neighbouring town to do the weekly shop and collect several weeks of child benefit. He left the house at around midday, and he re-emerged over twenty-four hours later, paralytic. He managed to gain entry through the front door, and his wife was anxiously waiting on the other side. He was so drunk that he lost his balance and fell on her, knocking her to the ground.

Jane had heard the commotion and started crying. Elizabeth was curled up in a ball on the floor, cradling her unborn child while praying it was unhurt and cursing her bloody selfish drunk of a husband. She managed to get up, holding on to the sideboard to steady herself. She couldn't bear to look at John, so she left him to it. She rang her babysitter asking if she would mind taking Jane and made her way to the hospital to get checked out.

She was seen quite quickly and told that she was very lucky, as apart from a few bruises there seemed to be no harm done. She took her time returning home. She really didn't want to have to deal with her husband in the state he was in.

All she really wanted was her daddy and for him to wrap her in his arms and tell her everything would be alright, but he was seventy miles away.

Elizabeth drove home, picking Jane up en route.

She carefully made her way up to the front door with Jane holding on tightly to her mother's hand. She turned the key and entered the cottage, which was in darkness. Her white cat, Arthur, was curled up asleep on the settee next to her husband, who was snoring loudly.

Elizabeth quietly made her way up the stairs. She put Jane to bed and then got undressed and took sanctuary in the double bed she usually shared with her husband. She closed her eyes and prayed John would have the good sense to stay out of her way and let her have some much-needed rest.

***

The following day dawned, and a very contrite John brought his wife breakfast in bed. He told her that he was thoroughly ashamed of his behaviour and pleaded with her to give him another chance. Elizabeth was still fuming, but her love for this man remained, with all of his many faults. He would have to cut down on the booze and start to take his responsibilities a bit more seriously. She ate the food that he had managed to prepare and watched him playing with his daughter, who he clearly adored. Could she trust him again? She wasn't sure, but she eventually gave him an exasperated hug and prayed that he would keep his word.

Over the next couple of weeks John barely left his wife's side. He was on his best behaviour and Elizabeth hoped the storm had passed.

On the 24th June Elizabeth went into labour again and their second daughter was born, weighing in at 8 lb 4 oz.

John was anxiously pacing the corridors waiting to be called in to meet the new arrival.

When he saw his exhausted wife holding their daughter in her arms, he felt huge relief, along with a great sense of shame as it hit him once again that his drunken behaviour could have damaged something so precious.

He held his daughter in his arms and looked down at her mop of dark hair and enormous blue eyes and just wanted to cry.

He really was trying to be a good husband and father.

The next day, when Elizabeth was discharged from hospital, Jane met her baby sister for the first time. She was rather intrigued by this noisy addition to the family, but she hoped that she wasn't going to cry all the time!

There was to be a family christening, as there had been for Jane. Elizabeth's parents and her Aunt Irene attended, but John's mother and sister declined the invitation as it was a longer trip for them, and they weren't very religious.

Elizabeth was very much looking forward to seeing

her family, particularly her father. Because the cottage was so small, Ben, Gwen and Irene had been booked into a local hotel.

The christening took place at the local church where Elizabeth played the organ. Reverend Jones arrived in plenty of time and had a little chat before the service began. He was elderly and going a bit deaf, and he was trying out his new 'all singing, all dancing' hearing aid for the first time.

The service was very pleasant, and all was going to plan until the vicar anointed Penelope. She was obviously not keen on water and proceeded to protest very loudly. Reverend Jones tried very hard to discreetly turn his hearing aid off while making a joke about the child's vocal abilities being a blessing in later life, with a bit of training.

The service ended and the family walked back to the cottage, where a typically English afternoon tea had been prepared. Deck chairs adorned the exceptionally spacious cottage gardens, which had been lovingly tended by George the gardener.

The sun shone on this pleasantly warm summer's day and the chinking of best china echoed on the warm breeze, along with the bell-like laughter that Gwen was known for. It was like a melodic vocal exercise and was highly infectious and a joy to the ear.

After they had finished their spread Ben decided that it was time for some family photos. He loved new gadgets and had just bought a Kodak Instamatic camera.

He insisted on taking a few more personal shots of Elizabeth and her two girls, as well as some involving everyone else.

They all had a simply fabulous day and Elizabeth was ecstatic. She loved her father so much, and she hugged him tightly as they prepared for their journey home. Standing in the driveway of their little cottage waving goodbye to her relatives brought a tear to Elizabeth's eye, which she wiped away briskly and managed a radiant smile as her father's car passed and disappeared up the hill and out of sight.

John put his arm around his lovely wife, and they went inside. After checking on the girls, the couple cuddled contently on the settee and finished the day off with a couple of glasses of wine.

They finally made their way up to bed around 11 p.m., having decided to leave the clearing up until the next morning. It had been an idyllic day in every way. Sometime later they fell asleep wrapped in each other's arms.

Chapter Four

The girls were growing up fast and although Penelope was very much in awe of her big sister, Jane was not so enamoured with her younger sister. She was used to being an only child and getting all the attention, so it was difficult adjusting to playing second fiddle.

Elizabeth, in the meantime, was plotting! The cottage was very crowded, and she'd heard through the village grapevine that the old seventeenth-century manor house, owned by a recently widowed elderly lady, might soon be on the market. The house had an annexe which had been added in the 1940s, used as a games room. Elizabeth knew exactly what she could use that room for.

She bided her time and spoke to her father about the possible purchase as Ben would have to act as guarantor for a mortgage. Ben wasn't sure about it, thinking the place was rather too large for the family's needs, but when Elizabeth discovered that she was pregnant again, he gave in. She was a difficult woman to say no to.

When she was five months pregnant, the house was theirs and they moved in. They bought a lot of second-hand furniture, including a beautiful Weber grand piano which would be housed in the old games room, now the music room.

The family had three cats and Elizabeth had her

dogs: a Great Dane called Sheba, and a lovely Golden Retriever called Pru.

Elizabeth's plans for the house were perfectly doable and would fulfil her creative streak, which she had had to put to one side whilst raising the children. The choir had dwindled somewhat, but she would soon sort that out! She had managed to continue with a bit of private piano tuition, which she planned to expand upon. Between accompanying other musicians and singers, going back to teaching in schools, hosting concerts in the music room and plans to set up a trust in aid of disabled children, there was plenty to keep her busy.

For the concerts John would act as mine host; doing his impression of Leonard Sachs from *The Good Old Days* would suit him down to the ground.

The house itself was stunning, steeped in history, from the wood-panelled dining room with its enormous fireplace, to the bedroom with its dressing room that Cromwell was supposed to have slept in. The front staircase led you into the lounge, which was filled with light from the generously sized windows, contrasting totally with the adjoining dining room, much darker because of the wooden panels. It had an anthracite boiler that was rather unreliable and open fires, which were much needed in such a large house.

It was a magnificent building but would be hellishly expensive to run, as the couple were well aware. Ben was waiting in the wings with his fingers crossed and a chequebook to hand!

The family had settled in nicely when the couple's

third baby made his appearance. He was the smallest of Elizabeth's brood, weighing in at only 7 lbs. Although it wasn't an easy birth, he was a very welcome addition and both Elizabeth and John were very happy to have a little boy.

He was named David and would be the apple of Elizabeth's eye.

Elizabeth had taken on an au pair and a number of cleaners (none of whom lasted long due to the size of the house).

She was keen to get on with her musical endeavours and when David was about a year old, she restarted her choral society. She had quite a few ladies of varying abilities but very few men.

Elizabeth decided to put on a well-known oratorio at the neighbouring village church and wanted her father to conduct it. She loved church music and was determined to lick the choir into shape. She started to have regular rehearsals on a Thursday evening and John would use this as an excuse to either go to the village pub or his golf club for a few drinks.

Elizabeth was just beginning a choir practice one evening when John arrived with a lady who he said he'd met at the pub and who was keen to join. Elizabeth put her in with the altos and didn't really pay her much attention at first as she was too busy focusing on the job in hand.

The lady, Julie, attended rehearsals regularly and when the practice was over, she and a few others would have a glass of sherry with the couple and then John would give a lift home to Julie and some of the others. By the time he returned, Elizabeth was usually spark out on the settee. It was a busy time for all of them.

The concert was a great success, and Elizabeth began making plans for the next choral society triumph.

Chapter Five

It took a few years, but Elizabeth's charity was finally flying high. She had gone to great lengths to set it up and now had a good team in place, as well as a well-known baritone and mezzo-soprano as their patrons.

Once a month they would fling open the doors of the music room for a charity concert, garnering rave reviews in the local newspaper for whichever 'stars' had trodden the boards that particular Saturday night. John was in his element as host, using his vast vocabulary to great effect, which was enthusiastically greeted with oohs and aahs.

The concertgoers were given a buffet and a glass of wine during the interval. The events became so popular that there was sometimes an overspill of people, and the doors to the glorious drawing room were opened to house a few extra chairs.

The performers usually stayed overnight, and Elizabeth and John were gracious hosts. They even had a bar installed in the lounge, where John enjoyed his role of barman.

In the 1970s everybody smoked, even the singers, and the lounge and dining room were thick with smoke, particularly in the winter, when opening any windows was foolhardy as preserving heat in such a large house was a necessity.

By this time, Julie had become good friends with Elizabeth and was the treasurer of the concerts' trust. She was about ten years younger than Elizabeth, dark-haired, olive-skinned and nearly six feet tall. She bought the children presents when she went away on business trips and Elizabeth felt a bit sorry for her as she thought she might be overcompensating because she was single and childless. Jane was quite keen on her, Penny less so and David pretty neutral.

Elizabeth had at one point tried to pair up Julie with a rather nice tenor soloist she knew, but there hadn't been a repeat performance after he gave her a lift home in his MG one night. In fact, he actively avoided her!

***

The two girls were doing well at school. Jane had her father's analytical mind, as well as having a gift for music, which of course came from her mother. She enjoyed school and was becoming a popular young lady.

Penny was shy and disliked large groups of people, blushing bright red if attention was drawn to her. She was not pretty in the conventional way but was very striking and had a kind nature. She was also very musical, which was to be her solace from an early age, as was her love of animals.

By this time, David was just starting school and struggled with reading, so he was sent for private lessons to a lady in the village. John was not happy that his son was not a mirror image of himself, and their relationship would always be turbulent. The problem wasn't in fact that 'the boy', as his father called him, was stupid, it was that he was dyslexic, something that was not widely known of in the 1970s.

Sheba the Great Dane had had two litters, each puppy selling for £50, and Elizabeth decided to buy an Apricot Miniature Poodle, who she named Lucy. Somewhat surprisingly, Lucy took a shine to Jane, who was not an animal lover. She was very clean and tidy and liked everything 'just so' and she had even started making her own clothes when she was just eight years old. She certainly didn't want animal hairs on any of her creations.

***

Life at the manor was chaotic. John worked from home but used to disappear to the local golf club or pub at the drop of a hat.

Elizabeth was so engrossed in trying to juggle her musical commitments, plus teaching at schools, private tuition and the choir, that by the end of each day she usually had a couple of sherries with the tablets she had recently started taking for her nerves. She fell asleep by about 10:30pm by the fire in the lounge, and when John did come home, he would have to wake her up in order for her to go upstairs to sleep.

The were becoming like ships in the night.

John was not particularly child orientated, given his own upbringing and apart from Jane, he had little time for this parenting lark. Elizabeth was now well into her forties and, having had four children, she had lost her lovely figure and the pills and drink weren't doing her looks any favours.

The couple's sex life was perfunctory at best. Elizabeth even confided in Julie as to her concerns over her deteriorating marriage. She was a very passionate woman and still had a high sex drive, but with an ever more absent husband she threw her excess energy into her music and children.

The concerts continued, as did the choirs. Elizabeth became increasingly ambitious, directing several oratorios, the biggest being *Elijah* with a Welsh National Opera baritone in the leading role and Penny making her debut in the role of 'the Youth'. It took place in a large round church with the soloists seated in the pulpit. Ben recorded the performance. It was a great success.

Penny had to sit on Elijah's lap until it was time for their 'duet'. When they rose to sing with each other, all you could see of her was the top of her head and a mass of thick wavy long hair and her eyes! With Elijah towering over her at 6 foot 4, it must have seemed quite amusing to the audience. Elizabeth praised her daughter's performance, as did Ben. But John said nothing.

Next, Elizabeth started a smaller choir, which Jane was a part of. There were only sixteen voices, and they were all cherry-picked.

David was sent away to boarding school aged eight. He hated school but he had to go somewhere, so it was decided to try a place in Nottingham to see if things improved for him. He had taken up the trumpet but seemed keen on percussion, particularly the drums.

Elizabeth missed her son terribly; John did not.

Julie was around a lot, and she and Elizabeth had grown quite close. The pair even went on a couple of weekend breaks to the Cotswolds. John and Elizabeth both drank far too much, but John would sometimes start before midday. He had a very short fuse at the best of times, but alcohol made him worse. When he came home and entered the house through the back door, his footsteps resounded loudly on the uncarpeted slabs leading through the corridor and dining room into the lounge. The sound made Lucy the poodle shake uncontrollably and bark incessantly, and if John ever made any attempt to approach her she would try and bite him.

Penny would come home from school at lunchtime and do some cheese on toast for her father and herself, and he was usually fairly affable at that point, but by the end of the day he could become extremely volatile. The children tried to avoid him in the evenings as he was pretty scary and would lash out verbally and physically for no good reason at all.

Elizabeth was beginning to wonder what on earth had happened to the man she had fallen in love with and married. They still slept in the same bed and she still *loved* him but she didn't *like* him very much any more. She knew that she was very busy with all her work and hoped that her husband didn't feel neglected, but he pooh-poohed this idea and said everything was just fine, and promptly disappeared to the pub!

Elizabeth was fast approaching her fiftieth birthday and the age gap between her and John was, in her head, becoming increasingly apparent; she felt old and frumpy. John had always been a bit of a flirt, but lately a dreadful feeling was growing day by day like a cancer.

One night John had said he was just popping to the club for a few drinks. It was an early summer evening and still light, and Elizabeth decided to follow him. She drove to the golf club and there was no sign of his car, so while she catastrophised internally she decided to drive to Julie's flat.

As she approached, she glanced up and through the half-closed curtains. She could see two people embracing. It was her husband and Julie.

She was hysterical as she managed to park her car and stagger up several flights of stairs. She pressed the doorbell and banged on the door, sobbing uncontrollably. By the time the door was opened she had collapsed, and an ambulance had to be called.

Elizabeth came round in a hospital bed to be told she had had a mild heart attack. John stood by her bed, playing the concerned husband.

She had very little fight left in her and was completely exhausted, but with her last bit of energy she raged at this man who had left her so broken, 'Get out you unfaithful bastard, get out!'

The nurse looked slightly embarrassed at the outburst, and John shuffled from one foot to the other, his head held too low for Elizabeth to catch his eye. She continued shouting at him and the nurse decided that it was best for all concerned if he left and they gave his wife a sedative to try and help calm her and hopefully let her sleep.

Elizabeth drifted into a fitful sleep, crying silently for a man who had never been worthy of her love.

Chapter Six

Having seen the doctor early the next morning, Elizabeth discharged herself from hospital. She ordered a taxi and stopped off at the nearest off-license and bought a large bottle of vodka.

John was very surprised to see her making her way up the driveway and through the front door.

He tried to speak to her, and she screamed at him and told him to get out. He said he had no idea why she was so upset and that she must calm down in view of her health. She raised her hand to slap him across his lying, hypocritical face, but he blocked her hand and she stumbled. He said there was nothing going on between him and Julie, nor any other woman. He said that Julie had just had some bad news and what Elizabeth had seen was him consoling her. He was a terrible liar and an even worse husband. She pushed past him, yelling, 'Liar! You unfaithful bastard!' repeatedly and made her way to their bedroom and slammed the door.

She rang her father who really had difficulty understanding his daughter as she was now sobbing uncontrollably. He suggested that perhaps she should come and stay with them for a few days and of course bring the girls, but Elizabeth declined. The conversation ended with Ben trying to reassure her that hopefully things weren't as bad as they seemed and that things would work out okay in the end, and various other platitudes. Elizabeth replaced the receiver and proceeded to pour herself a very large vodka and then she put a Shirley Bassey LP on the Dynatron full bore. By the time the song 'Born to Lose' came on, this highly intelligent, well-bred trailblazer of womankind was a crumpled wreck. Her expertly applied make-up was smudged, her carefully curled hair was limp, her pencil skirt was on skew-whiff, and she had alcohol stains on her pretty blouse. She had just staggered over to the Dynatron to put 'Born to Lose' on repeat and poured herself another large vodka when John made an untimely appearance, pleading with his wife to turn the music down. If looks could have killed, he would have died on the spot. She hurled her glass at him, narrowly missing and hitting the wall. He then made the mistake of entreating her to 'Calm down, lovey. Try to pull yourself together. You're making a fool of yourself.'

She screamed at him through a fresh flood of tears to 'get out', and mercifully he did the right thing for once and left her alone.

Elizabeth went to use the toilet and saw her reflection in the mirror. She tried to do something with her make-up but it was past redemption, so she took it all off and started again, a very difficult task when you're half-cut. Considering how many tears she had shed and how puffy her eyes and face were, she made a reasonable attempt and once she'd put a brush through her still-luscious locks, she didn't look too bad. She changed her blouse and straightened her skirt. Her armour was back in place.

She looked at her watch; the girls would be back from school soon. She turned the music down and decided to ring Julie. She was surprised when she answered as she thought she might still be at work. She used her best acting skills and her extremely upper-class clipped accent to disguise the fact she had been drinking, and she invited her around that evening for a chat. She said that they were all adults and needed to resolve this problem once and for all. Elizabeth suggested Julie called a taxi to arrive around six o'clock. Julie seemed affable enough and the trap was set.

The girls returned from school, Jane went and did her homework while Penny went straight into the music room to do some singing and dance practice.

Meals were rarely taken as a family. It was pretty much make-your-own and either eat it in the kitchen or sit with it on your lap in the lounge while watching TV.

At six o'clock precisely Julie made her way through the front gate and pressed the front doorbell. John had no idea that Elizabeth had invited her and as the two women entered the lounge, he realised his day was about to get a whole lot worse.

Elizabeth asked her husband to fix them all a drink, and once they were seated, she let rip.

'So, Julie, how long have you been screwing my husband for, hmm?'

John started to intervene. 'Steady on, Elizabeth.'

She glared at him and retorted, 'Shut up, you

unfaithful bastard. I wasn't speaking to you!' She continued with her verbal assault on Julie. 'Not only did you want to involve yourself in my entire life, but you wanted my husband too. Well, I'll tell you what, you two-faced bitch, you're welcome to him!' And with that she burst into tears.

The commotion had alerted the girls and they were sitting out of sight on the stairs, stifling giggles at the foul language, which was unheard of in this household, and the fact that their father had had sex – yuck! – and with someone else – even more disgusting.

Once more, John vehemently denied any wrongdoing, and Julie just sat there, looking extremely uncomfortable.

Elizabeth continued to rant at her husband, 'Don't you take me for a fool, you fucking bastard. Do you really think that I want you now, after you've been with *her*?'

At this point Julie had had enough and got up to leave, but Elizabeth pushed her back down onto the settee. 'I haven't finished yet, Julie.' Then she gestured towards John. 'You want him? Take him with you. You deserve each other!'

Julie stood up again and said to Elizabeth's husband, 'I don't want you, John. You can't afford me.'

What the hell did that mean? Jane and Penny were stunned, wondering what would happen next. Little did they realise that what was playing out in front of their very eyes would change the very fabric of their lives forever, and this moment would echo through time, wreaking havoc on all their plans, expectations and desires. They were watching the implosion of family life as they had known it. Nothing would ever be the same again.

Julie left under a tirade of abuse from Elizabeth, and John decided to make a sharp exit shortly after and hoped that his wife would calm down.

Elizabeth did quite the opposite. She went back upstairs to the bedroom and put her music on full blast. Several large vodkas later, having sobbed her heart out for over an hour, she passed out fully clothed on her bed.

The girls had kept their distance apart from Penny knocking once and getting no response. She decided it was probably best to leave her until the morning.

When John eventually returned home, the house was in darkness and so quiet you could have heard a pin drop. He decided that peace was just what he needed right now and made himself as comfortable as possible on the settee in the lounge, where Gladys, his favourite tabby cat, came and joined him.

Within ten minutes he was spark out.

The silence that then prevailed that night was most definitely the calm before the proverbial storm.

Chapter Seven

Elizabeth came round from her drunken slumber with an horrific hangover. As she staggered blindly into the bathroom she caught sight of herself in the mirror. A sob caught in her throat as she tried to stop the tears of utter dejection from pouring down her face. She was heartbroken, and judging by her reflection she was an old has-been too.

She drank a large glass of water with very shaky hands, and then she had a much-needed shower. The lukewarm water was quite a shock to her system and so she didn't linger. She then tried to do her make-up and hair, but yet again the tears started, and she had to keep stopping and taking it off as she looked horrendous.

'Bye, Mummy!' the girls shouted as they both went off to school. Elizabeth managed a rather shaky reply.

Luckily, she didn't have to go to work as the doctor had told her to rest for a couple of weeks following her health scare.

She finally managed to get dressed and was trying to do something with her hair when she heard the front doorbell go. Damn, who was that?

She then heard a rather adenoidal male voice and realised that it was Steve the piano tuner. Bugger, she could really do without him today, but she had two grand pianos, so he was going to be here for a while.

She knew her husband found him very irritating, so she left him to deal with him.

Elizabeth sat in her bedroom mulling over the events of the last few days, trying not to cry and really needing a 'hair of the dog'.

She needed to try and keep a clear head, at least for a while. She was deep in thought when John knocked on her door, softly saying her name, as if hoping by some miracle that she had amnesia and everything that had happened over the last few days had been magically erased from her memory. How wonderful that would have been for both of them, but this was real life, and it was a bitch!

'Get out, you unfaithful bastard!' Elizabeth shouted.

John made the mistake of rolling his eyes and saying, 'Please, love, not this again. I've explained everything—'

'Well, I don't believe you. You've been having an affair for years and I want you out of my house. How could you, John? You knew what I'd been through before we met.'

John couldn't meet her gaze. She was virtually unrecognisable from the woman he had married all those years ago, and he was responsible for her anguish. His selfish, egotistical behaviour had nearly killed his now, oh so fragile wife, but he wasn't going to come clean and be kicked out of his house. Oh no, he was sure that in time, he would win her round. He went to put his arms around her, to console her, but she pushed him away with all the force that her tiny frame could muster.

'Too little, too late, John. Now get out of my sight.'

He decided to leave her to it and went down to his office on the ground floor, where he had to endure Steve tuning the pianos to within an inch of their lives.

Penny came home from school for her lunch. She asked her father if he wanted some cheese on toast, and he said yes. As she could hear the piano tuner hard at it, she went through to the music room to see if he wanted a coffee. He said 'yes' and inquired as to how Elizabeth was, as he had heard of her health scare. Penny didn't really want to give out too much personal information, as Steve was also a piano pupil of her mother's and said that she was doing okay, but that she had been advised to take it easy.

After playing waitress to Steve and her father, Penny decided to check on her mother. She could even take her something to eat and sit with her for a while. She knocked gently on her bedroom door and was greeted by a rather subdued 'Who is it?'

Penny replied, 'It's me, Mummy. Can I come in?'

'Okay' was the reply, and she managed to juggle the plates and open the door without dropping anything.

Penny was taken aback by the look of pure and unadulterated misery on her mother's face. She put the food down and went over to Elizabeth and wrapped her arms around her, and the woman started sobbing so hard and clung to her daughter with all her might. She told her thirteen-year-old daughter that her father had been having an affair with Julie and that she hated them both and would never forgive them.

Penny was far too sensitive and much too young to deal with this kind of information or her mother's emotional state. She tried to get her to eat something, but to no avail and was concerned about leaving her and having to go back to school. She suggested maybe Elizabeth might pop over to see Jenny, their nearest neighbour, if she fancied a chat later on.

Elizabeth calmed down slightly and Penny felt it was safe to leave her. She gave her a quick hug and rushed back downstairs. She bumped into her father and shouted bye to him and to Steve, who by then was wandering around trying to find someone to pay his bill.

John wrote Steve a cheque and bundled him out of the front door as quickly as he could without causing too much offence.

He then went into his office and started typing a rather urgent letter to one of his most important clients.

Elizabeth, meanwhile, had resisted the urge to have any alcohol and decided that perhaps Penny's suggestion of dropping in on Jenny for some womanly advice was not such a bad idea.

She peered out of one of the front windows and saw her neighbour in the garden, so she made her way down the front staircase, through the front gate and just caught her as she was taking her shopping into the house.

Jenny could see that Elizabeth was in a terrible state and beckoned her into the inner sanctum of her home for a much-needed chat.

Jenny was a very attractive redhead with a slightly

older husband called Mike. They had two young children, who were both out with their father.

Jenny sat and listened to Elizabeth's tragic tale and her heart ached for this poor lady as she poured out her troubles. Obviously, the couples had socialised and Jenny had always found John to be a bit of a flirt. She hadn't thought anything of it though, as half of the male population of the village over the age of sixteen had a crush on her and so she wasn't short of admiring glances. But bringing a woman into your household, involving her in every aspect of you and your wife's lives – that was unbelievably callous.

Elizabeth was visibly shaking as she unburdened herself and Jenny considered offering her a stiff brandy, but it was only two o'clock in the afternoon so she made her a coffee instead.

Elizabeth asked Jenny what she would do.

Jenny was quite a straight talker when she needed to be, and although she was much younger than Elizabeth, by about sixteen years, she felt at that moment quite maternal towards her.

'Look, lovey, if I were you I'd stay put. Tell John to get rid of Julie and that she's never to darken your door again. Banish him to one of the spare rooms and try and carry on as best you can, for the sake of the children.'

Elizabeth thought about what her friend had said and agreed that it did make sense, but she didn't know how she would be able to cope with this sham of a marriage, feeling as heartbroken as she did.

Jenny told her to go home, tell John what she had decided, lay down the law, and take it one day at a time.

With that, she gave Elizabeth a warm, reassuring hug and sent her back over the road to her house. As she closed the door behind her, she hoped that her advice had been of value. Bloody men! Give them an inch!

Elizabeth entered through the front door and walked into the spacious lounge. She called her husband's name, and he made his way through the dining room to where she was waiting.

'I think we should sit down,' she said.

'Okay,' he replied, puffing nervously on a cigarette.

She then told him that he could stay, purely for the sake of the children, that he must never contact Julie again and that they would have separate bedrooms from now on.

Those were the terms, and if he didn't agree then he could go and pack now.

John acquiesced immediately to her demands.

Elizabeth walked back up the long staircase and through to what had been their marital bedroom.

She quietly shut the door, curled herself up into a tight ball and wept.

Chapter Eight

Jane was sitting on a coach at Reading station waiting to travel back home from a much-needed break with her grandparents. She had always loved staying with them in their beautiful house in the leafy suburb of Caversham.

They made her feel special, worthwhile, loved. It was a safe haven. She was quite content to sit doing her knitting, listening to *The Archers* with Ben and helping Gwen by carrying her shopping when they ventured into Reading.

Her grandparents were always thrilled to see their eldest granddaughter. She was growing up fast and had turned into a very pretty, intelligent and caring young lady.

She was studying for her O levels but was dreading the exams. She had a Mensa IQ, which her father boasted about incessantly, but she found writing an essay nigh on impossible and had to resort to asking her little sister for help.

Having been in the middle of her parents' recent marital bust-up, she had no intention of hanging around the 'family home' for any longer than legally necessary.

She had always seen the world through rose-tinted glasses, but the reality of her parents' behaviour lately had burst the bubble. Her father was a womaniser and her mother was drinking herself into an early grave.

She was sure that she wouldn't have behaved in such an undignified manner. In fact, no man would ever treat her with such disdain – she would make sure of that.

She had big plans. Once her exams were over, she was moving out and as far away from her selfish bloody family as possible.

The coach engine started up and she made herself comfortable for the journey home. With her latest knitting creation resting on the vacant seat beside her, she gazed out of the window at the passing countryside, lost in thought, and praying that perhaps, by some minor miracle, her parents might have calmed down and maybe even have patched things up.

On arriving back in Northampton Jane didn't bother telephoning her father for a lift. Instead she got herself a taxi back to the village.

As she opened the back door to the house she could hear her mother shrieking obscenities at her father like a banshee. She'd arrived home just in time for one of her mother's favourite lines: 'I am descended from the Earls of Cardigan, and you're just the son of a greengrocer!' Jane rolled her eyes. Oh great, just what she needed. *Hello, Jane. Did you have a nice trip? How are Ben and Gwen?* That would have been a 'normal' welcome and enquiry. She made her way up to her room, unnoticed.

She put her suitcase on the bed and decided that after she had unpacked and had a snack she would go round to a friend's house. Anything to escape the booming Dynatron blasting out yet another Shirley Bassey song and the constant slamming of doors and raised voices.

Having unpacked and changed her outfit, she surveyed her reflection in the full-length mirror. She applied a little mascara and a lip gloss and ran a brush through her light brown hair, which she wore in a stylish bob. She looked lovely, but she still wasn't satisfied. She made a mental note that she really must lose weight. She was very flat-chested and she thought her bottom looked enormous. There was no way that she wanted to be 'pear-shaped' or have 'childbearing hips', so she decided to do without the snack and make do with a few smarties. Eight, to be precise. She made a note of that and their calorific value.

She made her way downstairs in her platform shoes and out of the back door and walked up to the high street, where her friend Sally lived.

She knocked on the door and was relieved when Sally came and answered it with a big smile on her face.

The two girls went up to Sally's room and sat around chatting and listening to David Bowie. Jane didn't go into too much detail about her trip to her grandparents. That was her precious and private 'happy place'. She did, however, say that she had come home to World War Three, and no one had even noticed her return!

Sally rolled her eyes and made the right noises, but Jane knew she didn't really get it. She was putting on a brave face when her world was literally falling apart and the only person that she had to rely on was herself.

She was going to be so bloody perfect that she wouldn't ever let anyone in. The wall she was starting to build would be   impenetrable, so she laid back on her friend's bed, closed her eyes, and focused on the incredibly gorgeous voice of David Bowie, doing her best to block everything else out.

***

Jane managed to sit most of her O level exams, despite the ever increasingly alcohol-fuelled disturbances at home. Elizabeth's propensity for putting music on full bore while in the midst of one of her numerous dramatic episodes was leaving everyone fraught and sleep-deprived.

Everything was going downhill at an alarming rate and Jane could not wait to 'abandon ship'.

The day of her final exam (which was English) dawned. Her father had seen both girls go off to their respective schools, but Jane had decided that she couldn't bear to fail an exam and so she hadn't caught the bus. Her fear of failure was so intense that she couldn't take the risk.

With her parents being so self-absorbed in recent months, Jane thought that she would get away with it, but unfortunately, because of her exemplary attendance record, the headteacher telephoned her home and her father answered.

He later confronted her when she had sneaked home and was 'laying low' in her bedroom. John could not understand why his eldest child, who had a Mensa IQ, would be too scared to sit a basic O level. He was very disappointed in her.

The conversation was cut short by Elizabeth's return from work. John made a sharp exit, no doubt anticipating the usual tirade of abuse when his wife had consumed a couple of large orange juices, heavily laced with vodka.

Jane sat on her bed flicking through various magazines, looking at 'situations vacant' and came across a vacancy for an au pair needed to look after two young children in Cologne, Germany. She had only ever been abroad once, on a school trip to France, and she didn't speak any German, but she was looking for an escape route, so she put pen to paper, sealed the envelope, and having put a first-class stamp on it, popped out to post it while the coast was clear.

*****

Six weeks later Jane was living in a nice family home in Cologne. She had escaped! Jane had settled into her new job quickly and was proving to be very popular with the entire family.

She had a little self-contained annexe flat, which allowed her some much-needed privacy when she wasn't working.

She started exploring the local sights on her days off and also enrolled in a German language class.

The family's two little girls were becoming

increasingly fond of their pretty English nanny, who was also an extremely good role model for them. Jane was so relieved to be away from the bedlam of her parents' home that she found herself starting to relax a little and let her guard down. She even started to enjoy her food without counting calories and worrying so much about her figure.

Life in Germany was turning out to be just what she needed, until a couple of months into her contract she was rudely awoken by a familiar sound. Raised voices. As she came round from her sleep, she heard her employers at it 'hammer and tongs'. Hans was shouting and Clara was crying. Jane immediately tensed up and hoped they would calm down quickly and wouldn't involve her. She glanced at her watch; it was twenty past midnight. She hoped that the children hadn't been disturbed.

The row subsided within fifteen minutes, during which time Jane had put cotton wool in her ears and a pillow over her head to dampen the shrieking. She really didn't need this. She eventually managed to fall back into a fitful sleep.

Over the following months the rows continued, and Jane realised that Clara Fischer had an alcohol problem. Jane remained the 'model employee', but she had lost all respect for Clara. She had no intention of listening to and comforting another drunken middle-aged woman; she'd had quite enough of that in England. She did her job but withdrew into herself again.

She made acquaintances at her German class and was sociable when she got the chance to go exploring on the odd day off, but when she wasn't tending to the children she would go to her rooms and exercise frenetically, list calorific values of food, starve herself, then binge and purge. She read books, wrote letters to friends in England, knitted and started to plan her next move.

In seven months' time she would return to England, but she had no intention of ever living with her parents again.

She was making the most of the bad situation that she had found herself in but was counting the days until she could escape, yet again, from all of the mayhem.

***

John was looking forward to his eldest child's return from Germany. There were two rooms right at the top of the house that he had had decorated and made into a little apartment for her, thinking she might like to live more independently from the rest of the family now that she was nearly eighteen.

Elizabeth was drinking heavily and was having trouble holding down her teaching jobs, and the private sessions were becoming more and more erratic.

John kept his head down as much as possible and escaped to the golf club on a regular basis.

Whenever he returned, he knew there would be the usual scenario. Drunken accusations, loud music played sometimes until 3 a.m., and then she would pass out. The next day Elizabeth would be full of remorse, but that day would end up being a carbon copy of the previous one.

She was now a full-blown alcoholic, whose ability to function was greatly impaired.

John, however, was a functioning alcoholic (although he would never have admitted to it). A liquid lunch was becoming a regular thing. And so, the chaos continued.

The couple really had become a much more tragic version of Richard Burton and Elizabeth Taylor.

Jane had written a couple of letters to her parents, but neither had bothered to reply. However, John was pleased to note that Jane said that everything was going well, and that she would be returning to England in just under a month.

He continued with the decorating under the suspicious eye of his wife, who was so far gone that she seemed not to give a damn about their eldest daughter. This was something that saddened him greatly.

***

Jane's plane landed half an hour later than scheduled and she continued her journey home by taxi. She hadn't expected there to be anyone waiting at the airport to meet her, although she had given details of her flight in her final letter to her father.

As the taxi drove her through the pretty Northamptonshire countryside towards the family home, she wondered what kind of reception to expect. She would have dearly loved for it to have been something out of a fairy tale with a happy ever after, but she very much doubted that.

As the taxi pulled up outside the house, Jane took a deep breath, grabbed her bags, paid the driver and made her way up the gravel drive to the back door. As she entered, she was greeted by her father, who was not known for displays of affection (so a hug would have been out of the question), but he was smiling and seemed genuinely pleased to have her back at home.

Jane knew that she was going to have to be ruthless when it came to telling him that she was moving out, but she wouldn't tell him just yet.

They sat in the kitchen chatting about her trip and then Jane said she should really go and unpack. John told her about the rooms he had prepared for her, which caught her off guard and made her feel incredibly guilty.

She smiled and nodded and followed him up to the top floor. It was freezing cold, as most big old houses are, but he had thoughtfully put an old electric fire in her living room.

He left her to unpack and arrange things as she wanted. She was meticulously tidy, and everything had to be cleaned, washed, brushed and ironed to within an inch of its life. She hated anyone touching her things. Sharing was not something the children had ever been good at.

Later on, she heard the giveaway sounds of her

mother returning home: raised voices, loud music and doors being slammed.

Great, just what she needed!

She decided to stay in her 'flat' and try and avoid the inevitable drama. She would see if her mother was less inebriated in the morning.

Jane was weary from her journey and just wanted some much-needed rest. So, she got undressed and climbed into bed, with its freshly laundered sheets covered by a mountain of blankets and an enormous eiderdown. She closed her eyes and drifted into a deep sleep.

***

Early the next morning Jane saw her mother for the first time in over a year.

She had popped her head round her mother's bedroom door and was shocked by the deterioration in her appearance as she sat on the side of her bed trying to apply make-up with very unsteady hands.

She looked up to see her eldest daughter, who had a fixed smile on her pretty face, and nodded in her direction.

'So, you're back then, Jane. Did you enjoy your trip?'

Jane started to tell her about the two little girls that she had been looking after, but she noticed how Elizabeth's eyes glazed over and so she decided not to waste her breath, giving her a brief hug and saying that she had to rush or she would miss her bus. Her mother didn't even reply.

Jane didn't bother to eat breakfast. She'd taken a good hard look at herself in a full-length mirror and had decided that her 'enormous bottom' had to go.

She was rushing down the back staircase trying to remember the calorific value of a piece of cheesecake when she bumped into her younger sister.

'It's been hell here,' Penny told her. 'You wouldn't believe how bad it's got.'

Jane frowned. 'I think I've got a pretty good idea. Mummy looks terrible. Must dash. I'll see you later!'

'Oh, okay,' said Penny, somewhat taken aback as she watched her sister disappear down the road to the bus stop.

Jane had decided to keep her moving-out plans to herself, so the fewer people who knew what she was planning the better.

The bus arrived on time and Jane found herself a seat and gazed out of the window daydreaming, until she was brought back down to earth with a bang when the bus pulled in at the bus station. It had a terrible reputation and was full of pervy old men and the 'special brew' brigade. She exited the bus and hastened her pace to get back out into the fresh air as quickly as possible.

She'd arranged to meet Sharon outside Wallis, and she did a spot of window shopping while she waited. Sharon eventually arrived 'fashionably late', and they made their way to a local café. Sharon ordered toast and pastries. Jane resisted until she saw the cheesecake and then caved in. One small slice of cheesecake couldn't do too much harm – she'd do without any tea.

Sharon told her the name of the 'man with a van' who would move her stuff to her new flat in the town centre in just over four weeks' time.

Jane was very excited but knew all hell would break loose at the family home. She couldn't stay in the middle of the countryside, even if things had been okay at home. She needed to get on with her life. She had ambition and she needed to succeed and that meant that she had to make this change. It was no big deal in comparison to getting on a plane to another country for a year. She wasn't afraid of being on her own. She was extremely self-sufficient and capable. She had to look after number one.

***

Jane stared at the ceiling of the bedroom of her new flat. She was exhausted, both physically and emotionally, but she'd done the hard bit, she'd broken free. No more screaming and shouting. She might actually get a decent night's sleep now.

Her thoughts drifted back to the previous day and to The Move. She knew how much she had hurt her father and she felt as guilty as hell, but it was done now, and she tried to erase the image of his anguish as he realised that there was nothing that he could do to stop his daughter from leaving. Her mother had been more interested in ranting and raving at him as per usual, rather than being bothered by Jane's departure.

She got up and nipped to the bathroom to use the loo, and then she set about making herself a hot drink while putting the rest of her belongings into their allotted places. When she had finished unpacking and tidying up, she had a lovely hot shower and got dressed.

As she was finishing blow-drying her hair the doorbell went, and she looked out of the window to see Sharon waiting outside, as they'd arranged.

The two girls linked arms and made their way into the town centre, where they could sit, chat and people-watch. It wasn't long before they were being badly chatted up by two opportunistic young men. Jane was pleasant enough to them, but she was not in the least bit interested. Sharon, however, had different ideas and Jane was left to walk home alone. Typical!

On arriving back at her flat she started sorting out her work clothes as she was starting her new job as regional manager the following day. She had a new store to window-dress in Birmingham and she went to bed looking forward to her new challenge and her new life. She'd checked the train times and set her alarm for 6 o'clock in the morning. She spent the rest of the evening doing some knitting and watching a bit of TV.

That night she slept more soundly than she had done in years.

The new shop was a huge success and Jane received high praise from her boss at HQ. After a week of early starts and commuting back and forth to Birmingham she was quite tired, but she had already decided that she was going to visit her grandparents as she was becoming concerned about Grandpa's stomach ulcer. She knew it was making his general health quite fragile, along with his advancing years and the stress of Elizabeth's problems, particularly her drunken volatile behaviour.

Jane phoned her grandparents from the public phone in the hall and said that she would drive down the next day and to expect her around lunchtime. Grandpa's voice sounded weaker than it usually did, but she couldn't talk for long as she was running out of change to feed the payphone.

She went back into her flat and started packing a small bag for her trip. This would be the first time that she had driven to Berkshire. She had kept her driving lessons a secret and passed her test first time. She had managed to buy a cheap second-hand car, which was waiting at the garage for her to collect first thing in the morning. Organised was her middle name. She climbed into bed having set her alarm and drifted off into a much deserved and needed sleep.

Chapter Nine

Jane headed for the motorway the next morning. She was a confident driver, with a very good sense of direction. She turned the radio up and sang along with her favourite pop songs.

The traffic wasn't particularly heavy and there were no hold-ups or diversions and so she arrived at her grandparents about half an hour earlier than she had anticipated. She hoped that one or both of them would be in as she was in urgent need of the loo.

She rang the bell and Gwen answered quite quickly. She greeted Jane with a loving hug and her bell-like laughter. She shouted to her husband 'Ben! Ben! Jane's arrived. You stay where you are, we'll come through.'

Jane followed Gwen through to the living room, which was thick with smoke due to Ben's sixty-a-day habit. The number had increased since macular degeneration had robbed him of the majority of his sight.

He stood waiting for the pair to enter the room. He was six feet tall but was stooping more than the last time Jane had visited. They embraced and he then sat back down again in his chair next to his old-fashioned radio, which was now his only connection with the outside world, aside from the telephone.

Jane looked at the cigarette burns in the armchair,

where he now spent most his life. He had missed the ashtray, which was full of cigarette ends. She waited until her grandfather had finished smoking and duly emptied it. Gwen bustled about, preparing lunch and singing happily to herself, while Jane gave a helping hand and chatted to Ben. She told him that her flat was very cosy and that she was really enjoying work.

The three of them had a nice lunch, but Ben hardly touched his food. Jane knew it was because his stomach was too painful, but he tried to make light of it. He was incredibly thin. He had always been slim, and of course his smoking didn't help.

Jane helped Gwen with the washing up, and the telephone rang just as they had finished. Gwen went into the hall to take the call, and from her grandmother's side of the conversation Jane guessed that it was Elizabeth.

Her grandmother returned to the living room looking a little agitated and Jane prayed that her mother wasn't going to start ringing incessantly, as she knew how upsetting this would be for her grandparents. They were too old and frail to have to cope with her drunken episodes. Jane thought her to be very selfish. Why the hell couldn't she pull herself together, stop drinking, or just leave her father? It was such a mess.

The remainder of her visit was uninterrupted, mercifully. They all attended church the following day, where they were warmly received. There was a real sense of community in this church and Jane was introduced, enthusiastically by her proud grandfather, to anyone who had not met her before. After the service had finished, she was complimented on her lovely singing voice. They were dropped back at the house by a member of the choir, and Gwen and Jane finished off preparing Sunday lunch. Again, Jane noticed how little Ben ate, pushing his food around the plate to make it look as though he had eaten something, by merely rearranging it! It was at times like this that you could really do with a dog, which you could feed under the table (which was something she and her sister had done many a time, with some of the burnt offerings their parents had dished up over the years!).

Jane helped with the drying up, and with a heavy heart packed her overnight case and put it into her car.

She gave her grandparents a hug and tried not to well up as she waved goodbye as they stood on their doorstep arm in arm, the perfect devoted couple waving goodbye to their much-loved granddaughter.

As Jane made her way back to Northampton, she still felt the lovely warm glow that only her grandparents could give her. It was a sense of being truly loved and accepted for who she was.

She hoped that Ben's health wouldn't deteriorate any further. She really did not know how she would cope without him.

Chapter Ten

Elizabeth was no longer able to work, and John's business wasn't exactly thriving. Ben had been helping out with the mortgage repayments but had finally put his foot down. They had no choice but to sell up.

They moved to a six-bedroom semi-detached house on a main road in the town, opposite the park. Penny hated it and David just went to school (or not) and kept out of the way.

Elizabeth went into rehab for a couple of weeks and on her return was very quiet and withdrawn. She soon started drinking again and it was hell for everyone concerned, especially the new neighbours, who could hear all the commotion through the adjoining walls.

Jane called round shortly after they had moved in. She was on her way back from a promotional job that she was doing. She was looking very chic when she knocked on the door of the new 'family home'. Her father of course was pleased to see her, but she was met with great hostility from her mother. She flinched inwardly and tried to maintain her composure as she sat gingerly on the edge of an armchair that was covered in cat hairs. Out of politeness she managed to stay for half an hour, but then she fled.

On returning to her flat, she devoured a large bar of chocolate followed by an enormous chunk of cheesecake. She then went to the loo and stuck two fingers down her throat.

She felt terrible. She must be more controlled. She was too fat. She had to diet and stick to it rigidly.

She took her make-up off, cleaned her teeth and climbed into bed. The warm, loving glow of belonging and being protected had been replaced with the reality of self-loathing and complete and utter misery. She hated crying as she thought it showed weakness, but she did cry that night. She cried for a mother who she no longer had, and for the 'perfect little family' that she thought she had when she was a little girl, but which in reality had never existed.

***

Jane was extremely determined. She knew that there were certain things that she had to achieve to become as perfect and indispensable as she needed to be. First, there was the dieting. She now had that firmly under control, regularly weighing and measuring herself, overexercising and if she did happen to 'fall off the wagon' she found that laxatives worked very well in stopping any weight gain and keeping a nice flat stomach.

She also decided that she needed cosmetic surgery. She did have slightly protruding ears and was not happy that, with the best will in the world, her fine hair in a lovely 'bob' could not disguise this imperfection. She was doing promotional work now. She couldn't have sticky-out ears, so she made inquiries, found a surgeon, borrowed some money from her grandfather, and without telling anyone (except Sharon), she had otoplasty as a day procedure and took a week off work to recover. She was in quite a lot of pain but the procedure went well, and she was thrilled with the result. Next on her list was a nose job. She had a bump on her nose, and it didn't photograph well, but she would have to save up for that. In the meantime, she went back to work. She was always at the front of the queue for any extra work, not one to miss out on opportunities. She was a hard taskmaster and couldn't stand slackers.

She had her eye on a nice flat. She had a boyfriend. He was highly unsuitable. Much older, married, but prepared to indulge her, and either too self-absorbed or too thick (or both) to be concerned about her increasingly obsessional behaviour whether it be binging or laxative abuse.

She was very domesticated and loved cooking (for other people). She was the perfect hostess: pretty, intelligent, a good listener. She could be quite sociable but was equally happy sitting doing her knitting, watching the television alone. She didn't drink or smoke but didn't seem to mind if others did.

She occasionally called in to see her father, but her visits were always upsetting and toxic.

Her brother had now flown the nest, and Penny was the 'last man standing'. She'd been working in a theatre production for a few months but when her contract ended she'd returned to the 'family home' and eventually found herself a job that she hated. She was suffering with anxiety and the beginnings of an eating disorder. All the screaming and shouting over the years had left her a nervous wreck. Jane didn't know why she stayed. She felt sorry for her little sister and had a word with her head office in London and managed to get her an interview for a concession in a shop in the town centre. 'Don't mess it up,' she warned her Penny, 'or show me up!'

Jane was amazed and secretly delighted when Penny not only got the job but became one of the best managers she'd ever had, highly praised by Terri at HQ.

Phew! That was a relief, one less thing to worry about, and it seemed that Penny had found something else she was good at apart from singing.

Penny had a bedroom right at the top of the house and when she went to work each day, she would lock her door. On her return her mother was always drunk, spoiling for an argument and so Penny just went out more and more frequently. She started inquiring about rooms to rent and went to look at a house share but didn't hear anything back.

One night she came home and found that Elizabeth had been in her room (she must have forgotten to lock it) and emptied all of her clothes into black bin bags, which she had strewn all over the landing. She was furious and an almighty row ensued. Penny stormed out of the house and walked round the block to try and calm down, but when she returned, she found her mother (who was so drunk she could barely stand) screaming at her father about his affair, and he was about to hit her. She got between her parents, crying, imploring them to 'stop it!', at which point her mother stumbled back into her bedroom and her father went back to his relative safe haven, his library.

The following day Penny found herself a bedsit and on the next payday she took her few belongings and fled. Her father's harrowing cries rang loudly in her ears: 'That's right! You fucking well leave me too!'

She now had a cold downstairs room with an electricity meter, a bathroom and toilet which she shared with five other people – and if you wanted a bath you had to put a note on the door and money in that meter too! She didn't have a TV and had to pop round to a friend's to watch *EastEnders* and *Top of the Pops*.

Her eating disorder meant that it didn't matter that the fridge was empty. Her eating had become quite chaotic. She had been taking tips from her big sister, especially on the laxative front.

She would meet up with Jane over work issues and she would sometimes pop round to her sister's nice new flat, but she wasn't keen on Jane's boyfriend, who was ancient and extremely uncouth.

Penny started seeing someone. He used to turn up on a Friday night, stay the weekend and disappear back on the road on Sunday night. They had nothing in common, but Penny would get drunk to try to fit in.

One Saturday morning, about six months after Penny had left home, her father came knocking on the front door. He told her that Grandpa had passed away the previous day. He had just been to tell Jane. He said he would let them know about the funeral arrangements. As Penny went to see her father to the door he said, 'Why don't you come home, lovey? You don't want to live like this.'

She felt her eyes well up with tears, but she blinked them back and shook her head and said she was fine living where she was.

It was a very sad day for both of the girls. They were heartbroken. Penny was riddled with guilt as she hadn't visited Ben in two years, and Jane had had such a wonderful relationship with her grandpa over the years. She was inconsolable.

***

The congregation of the mourners rose as indicated by the Baptist minister, and Ben's coffin was carried into the church by the pallbearers and set down by the altar.

Gwen stood next to Jane, her gloved hand grasping her hanky, just in case 'the stiff upper lip' should buckle and she should cry, heaven forbid. Her only consolation in losing her beloved husband of nigh on sixty years was her unerring belief that he was now with Our Lord Jesus Christ. She sang all the hymns with gusto, as if she knew that he could hear her. He had always loved her beautiful voice. Penny stood next to her elder sister, looking anxious and trying not to cry. She was an extremely emotional girl.

The day had started badly: when she had arrived at her parents' house dressed in black she'd been told to 'get changed immediately' by her father, because 'people don't wear black to funerals these days.' She fled back to her bedsit in tears and found a different skirt, but the drive to Reading had been fraught and she had sat in the back of the car in total silence. Elizabeth was forced to beg her husband for some alcohol when they arrived at her parents' house, as her breakfast dose had worn off and she was shaking uncontrollably. Jane was disgusted by her mother's behaviour and had little time for her these days. Gwen was appalled at her daughter's appearance and behaviour, despite having been on the receiving end of her drunken calls to the house at unearthly hours for the past few years.

When they arrived at Gwen's she had Jean – a family friend who was also Ben's secretary – with her for moral support. Jean travelled in the family car to the church and sat in the pew behind Gwen. As they listened to the minister reading the eulogy, Jean placed a reassuring hand on Gwen's shoulder.

Penny just wanted to open the coffin and rescue her grandpa. She couldn't cope with any of this, and although she was surrounded by people, she felt very alone.

The church was packed, of course, and everyone was invited back to the house for the wake. The spread had been prepared earlier by Irene, Jean, Gwen and Marjorie (Gwen's cleaner). Jane helped play hostess with her grandma and great aunt Rene (Ben's sister), handing out sandwiches and making small talk.

Penny sat in the kitchen, hoping nobody would bother her. She was upset. Why was everybody chatting and laughing? It didn't seem right to her. Grandpa had just been buried.

Elizabeth managed to stay relatively sober and not start a slanging match in the middle of the wake. She was staying on with her mother to help sort out the sale of the house, and then Gwen was going to be coming to live with them in Northampton.

On the return journey, Jane sat in the passenger seat and Penny, again, sat in virtual silence in the back.

Jane made conversation with her father and instructed him on the route home as he was an atrocious driver with absolutely no sense of direction – rather ironic for someone who used to be a driving instructor.

Finally John pulled up on the drive, and the family members all went their separate ways. No hugs, no words of comfort. Family in name only.

'Dysfunctional' didn't even begin to cover it.

***

Gwen moved to Northampton several weeks later. John had enjoyed the relative peace of not having Elizabeth in the house but knew that this would be the calm before the storm. Gwen was given the single bedroom next to the bathroom on the first floor – unfortunately next to her daughter's bedroom. Her son-in-law slept in a room at the top of the house (out of harm's way).

Gwen had lived a very sheltered life. She was

extremely religious and had been a devoted wife to Ben for sixty years. She had never had to deal with anything other than cooking, a little light housework and playing hostess for her husband's business dinners, particularly in the early days of their marriage. Now everything she had ever known and loved had been wrenched from her. Ben, her home, friends from church, and she had been uprooted and brought to live with her alcoholic daughter and adulterous son-in-law. She felt so lost, alone, and so frightened.

The constant alcohol-fuelled slanging matches and Elizabeth's volatile behaviour were so alien to Gwen. It was so unlike anything she had ever experienced that her health began to deteriorate. Granted she was in her eighties, but before she moved in with her daughter she had been reasonably healthy, apart from being slightly deaf.

She didn't recognise this woman that she had given birth to. God knows they had never been close, but she found herself becoming more and more dependent on her son-in-law. He seemed to be the lesser of two evils.

John did make an effort to take Gwen to the local church a few times but he wasn't the most reliable chauffeur, so eventually Gwen had to make do with sitting in the lounge singing along with the hymns on *Songs of Praise* on a Sunday night. A poor substitute for all her church friends and the services and sermons that had given her succour in her times of need for so many years.

Penny visited Gwen regularly, and even became her

hairdresser. She would give her grandma a perm, or a wash and set, then dry her hair and style it, and when she was trying to make her laugh, she would put a tea cosy on her head. It had the desired effect. At least it had made her smile. Gwen asked her a couple of times if she could come and live her, but Penny explained that her bedsit wasn't really suitable. Knowing only too well what living in that environment was like, Penny's heart went out to her.

David had called in on a rare visit and Grandma had still been in bed. The usual sniping was ensuing between his parents and as he passed Gwen's room, he caught sight of her putting her teeth in, and heard her repeating again and again 'How dare you. How dare you' at the profanities that assaulted her senses. Jane visited a little more regularly and tried to take Grandma out occasionally, but it was becoming increasingly difficult.

Then, not many months after the move, Gwen suffered a mild stroke and became reliant on a wheelchair for any outings. It was also becoming clear that she was suffering from dementia. She kept asking Penny if she could move in with her and her husband and three children. At first Penny tried to correct her but eventually, realising that this scenario seemed to make her grandma happier, she just smiled and nodded when she asked how her children were, and she would tell Gwen that they were all well.

She became less and less lucid, and it was as though she had retreated into a safer place, away from the harsh realities that she had found herself living in, and sadly, within the year, she too had passed away, perhaps willing herself to die to be with her beloved Ben and Jesus Christ her saviour.

John attended her funeral with Jane, but Penny and David refused to go, and Elizabeth was too far gone to even know what day it was, let alone that her mother had died.

Jane exuded respectful attention as the pastor said a few words about Gwen, a woman he had never met. She felt a mixture of relief that her grandma was finally away from the sheer hell that she had had to endure for the final year of her life, and a deep longing to be back with her grandparents in their house in Reading, and to feel that warm glow of love one last time.

Chapter Eleven

Jane had learnt at quite a young age that keeping busy blocked out a lot of emotional trauma. She was doing really well in her various jobs and had decided that she needed a new look to go with some promotional work she had lined up, so she decided to have a day out in London and invited Penny to tag along. She had a busy schedule. She was having her hair permed at a well-known hair salon and also doing some retail therapy, before popping in to see her boss in Great Portland Street.

Jane drove to London. Penny was really impressed by her driving ability, nothing seemed to faze her.

Jane had been to this particular hair salon once before so she knew what to expect. But what she wasn't expecting was for Penny to completely steal her thunder with her incredibly thick and wavy waist-length auburn hair. At one point she had five hairdressers playing around with it. They ended up washing it and putting it in massive rollers to straighten it and give it a lift. The result was fantastically shiny, bouncy hair, and Jane's perm added some volume to her finer hair.

Jane then did her clothes shopping. She had expensive taste.

Penny was broke, but she was happy enough window shopping while her sister spent her hard-earned cash.

They then called in to see Terri, their boss. Penny had

only ever spoken to her over the phone until then, and they got on like a house on fire in person, which pleased Jane.

There was just one more port of call before returning home: Jane had a consultation with a cosmetic surgeon regarding her rhinoplasty. She wanted the bump removed from the bridge of her nose. Penny sat in the palatial waiting room thumbing her way through a copy of *Harpers and Queen* until her sister reappeared, delighted with her consultation. The surgery was scheduled for in a month's time.

Penny was in total awe of her sister. The two girls were like chalk and cheese and Penny wore her heart very much on her sleeve. She was way too emotional for Jane's taste, but on this occasion they were both pleased with how their day out together had gone. It was something of a rarity, but it had been productive – and Jane was happy to see her sister smiling for once. She dropped her off at her bedsit and sped off back to her flat.

Her boyfriend had left a message on the answering machine about calling round later, but she was tired, so she put him off and tried on all of her new clothes once more before she got herself ready for bed. She had an early start, so she set her alarm and fell asleep feeling quite contented.

***

The long-awaited nose job had finally happened, and Jane was taking time off work while all the bruising reduced and her new nose healed. It was incredibly painful, she couldn't breathe properly and her nose had been packed with gauze for the first day post-op in order to stem the bleeding. When they removed the gauze it felt as though they were pulling her brains out. She begged the nurse to stop, but it had to be done. Christ, she prayed this was all going to be worthwhile, and that the outcome would be what she had dreamt about for so long.

It was. She now had a diminutive nose that suited her face beautifully. It was perfect, and Jane couldn't wait to get some promotional photos done to add to her CV. She had changed her hair colour to a reddish brown, and she just had to keep up with her strict dieting, exercise regime and laxative use. She thought she was making great strides in becoming the girl she'd always wanted to be. After all, 'no pain, no gain'. She should have that tattooed on her arm.

She hadn't seen her father since her operation, and as going to the family home was never a joyous event, she kept putting it off. However, after an absence of several months she felt obliged to make a call. She was immaculately turned out as she parked her little car outside and strode up to the front door with a cheery smile fixed on her face.

The door was answered by Elizabeth, who scowled at her eldest child and left her standing in the hallway as she staggered off to get herself a large vodka. Her father was dozing in his armchair in the lounge with Penny's cat, Skinner, asleep on his lap and a half-drunk tumbler of whisky on the occasional table. He started as Jane entered the room and after muttering 'Hello, lovey' he disappeared to the loo.

Oh, how delightful, thought Jane. *Nice to see you too.*

John reappeared and asked her if she wanted a cup of tea. She followed him into the kitchen, which was an absolute tip, and opened a few cupboards in the vain hope of finding a clean cup and saucer. Eventually she succeeded and decided that a black tea on this occasion was probably safest and less likely to give her salmonella. As she followed her father back into the lounge her shoes were actually sticking to the dirt on the kitchen floor. The place was a health hazard! Before she sat down, she produced some Sellotape from her handbag and started to remove the cat hairs, and it was at this point that Elizabeth decided to reappear. She staggered through the doorway and plonked herself onto the settee in a very unladylike manner. She glared at her husband and then, having given her daughter the once over, said, 'You look different.'

Jane replied in a slightly flustered way, 'Yes, Mummy. I've changed my hair colour. Do you like it?'

Elizabeth rose very unsteadily and hovered over her daughter in a most alarming manner. Jane wriggled uncomfortably in her seat. The smell of alcohol and smoke were pungent, but her mother's bloated appearance and the way she was peering at her was even more unnerving than usual.

Elizabeth finally remarked, 'I know what it is. You've had your nose made smaller. I always wanted mine done.' With that, she burst into floods of tears and staggered back upstairs to console herself with another large vodka. Her father winced as he picked up his whisky and yet again Jane wondered why on earth she had bothered to visit.

She left shortly after, as her father had turned on the TV for the snooker and she was just sitting there, surplus to requirements. He raised his hand in a rather lame wave goodbye as she took her leave and rushed outside to her 'getaway car'. From outside she still hear her mother shrieking. What a bloody madhouse. Even her daddy couldn't be bothered with her any more.

On her return to her flat she demolished a giant bar of chocolate followed by several pastries and a gateau, washed down with a packet of laxatives. She thought she'd looked really nice today, but she'd been invisible to her parents. Her mother was vile and jealous, and her father was a pathetic drunk.

She spent most of the night on the toilet. She woke the next day and after weighing herself decided that she had to embark on an even stricter eating regime. That would make everything better again.

***

The retail company that Jane was area manager for was closing a few branches, one of which was the one Penny ran. Terri at head office had asked her to move to London, but she wasn't interested. She got a good reference and managed to get a manager's job elsewhere, but it soon became clear that she was out of her depth. She was much younger than the other managers and not suited to working for a large organisation. She lasted three months and ended up seeing the doctor, who decided she was suffering from depression and put her on medication. The pills made her ill; she had been feeling anxious about not having a job, but she was now unable to leave the house. Jane tried to rally round and help her sister but she feared Penny was having some sort of breakdown. After coming off the drugs, Penny became much more reclusive and started starving herself as punishment for her perceived failure.

In stark contrast, Jane's luck had picked up and with her new look, she had managed to land herself an evening job doing promotional work, which involved travelling round to pubs within about a 40-mile radius.

Mike, Penny's boyfriend, was at a bit of a loss, not really being able to cope with her fragile mental health. When Jane asked if he would act as her 'bodyguard', he jumped at the chance, particularly as she was now driving an Mazda RX-7 sports car, and of course being seen out with an attractive woman was always good for the ego. So, win—win really!

Penny said she really didn't mind or care, so most Friday and Saturday nights, Jane got dolled up, turned up at her sister's bedsit and sped off with her sister's boyfriend in the passenger seat. This continued for a couple of months. Jane still had her day job, so she didn't have much time to think about anything other than work.

She would occasionally pop in on her sister, who was losing weight at an alarming rate now. Jane didn't really know how to deal with her overly emotional sister. God, she was becoming like her mother!

Jane's boyfriend had had enough and disappeared off the scene. Again, this didn't really bother her. There was always another man hanging around her. Well, she wasn't exactly ugly.

She'd been working all week and normally she would do the pub run with Mike at the weekend, but she'd been invited to a friend's birthday bash, so she took the weekend off. She told Mike that she wouldn't be needing him but hoped he'd be available for the following weekend. He decided to get a few beers in and watch some TV with his increasingly distant girlfriend.

Jane took one last look in the full-length mirror in her bedroom. She was wearing a blue jumpsuit that she had made herself, and she had tied her dark auburn hair loosely back. She still wasn't happy with her figure, but she was getting there. Anyone looking at her would see a stunning, confident woman, and it's true that she knew she was a head-turner. However, beneath that confident façade lay a broken little girl who, unlike her sister, rarely showed her emotions.

Jane arrived at the party around nine o'clock and mingled quite happily as she knew the group of people and felt very much at ease. The only drink she had was a white wine spritzer, which she nursed all night. She didn't like alcohol.

Jane left the party shortly after midnight. She'd had a

busy week at work and didn't want to be too late home. She decided to take the scenic route and turned up the radio as she drove along the almost deserted back roads, which she knew like the back of her hand. As she approached a very tight double bend, she was momentarily blinded by the headlights of another car that had seemed to come from nowhere. She slammed on her brakes and the car left the road and crashed headlong into a brick wall.

She lay like a rag doll slumped over the steering wheel, the car crushed around her limp body. It took the fire crew well over an hour to rescue her and they hadn't anticipated anyone surviving given the state of the car. She was taken by ambulance to the nearest hospital and was put on the critical list in intensive care. Her life was hanging by a thread.

***

John was woken from his slumbers at about 2 a.m. on a Saturday morning to be informed that his eldest child had been in an horrific car crash and was fighting for her life in intensive care at a hospital 15 miles away. He stumbled about in a blind panic, trying to get dressed and also trying to explain to Elizabeth the gravity of the situation. Elizabeth wasn't interested, which shouldn't really have surprised him, but even in her permanently drunken condition he would have hoped she would have felt something; after all, Jane was her child too.

He drove alone to the hospital. He was a bad driver

at the best of times so he was glad that he at least knew the route.

On arrival he explained who he was to the nurses on reception and was taken up to intensive care. The nurse who accompanied him gently warned him that his daughter was hooked up to all sorts of machines but that she was in the best possible place, and he should try not to get too distressed.

As he entered the room, the nurse who had been checking the monitors moved discreetly away and left the room, indicating that she would be just outside if she was needed.

John's face was ashen as he beheld the extent of the trauma that his child had suffered. All he could see was a fragile young woman, with tubes coming out of everywhere, fighting for her life. He'd not been a good father, he knew that. He was weak and pathetic, but he loved this girl with every ounce of his being and had never told her so. He didn't know how.

He sat wearily on one of the chairs in the room and wept quietly for several minutes until a nurse reappeared to check on Jane. She put a reassuring hand on his shoulder and suggested that he wait outside in the corridor and that when there was any news she would come and find him.

He was not a particularly religious man, but that night he prayed to God to save his daughter. She had so much to live for and was far too young to die.

***

Jane's eyes began to flicker as she started to come round. She could hear people saying her name but she had no idea what was going on. Then she heard a familiar voice – her father's. She started to tremble and cry uncontrollably. Her father's voice became clearer: 'You're in hospital, Jane. Try and calm down, lovey. You had a car accident.'

She tried to move and then became aware of all the machinery that she was hooked up to. She tried to speak, but her jaw was too painful. What the hell had happened to her? She just wanted to escape, but there was no escape route.

Jane was not going to be an easy patient; she was in a lot of pain, she had a broken leg and arm and had broken her jaw. She was on very high doses of morphine to help her deal with her injuries, but ultimately she was going to have to have her jaw wired shut under general anaesthetic. The maxillofacial consultant was eager to get the surgery over with as it would ease Jane's pain and also her mounting anxiety, but they had to be sure that she was strong enough to withstand the procedure.

John had stayed by his daughter's bedside apart from popping home a couple of times for a shower and a change of clothes. He had even kept his alcohol intake to the bare minimum. He had to be there for his daughter in her hour of need.

On the day of the surgery, he watched as her trolley was pushed down the corridor towards the theatre. He muttered, 'Chin up, lovey' and immediately regretted doing so, but that had been the best that he could muster in these stressful circumstances.

He sat and waited in a side room out of public view, alone with his thoughts. He really could have done with a drink, but he resisted yet again. Remaining relatively sober was the least he could do for his little girl, with all that she was going through.

He was beginning to doze, snoring softly, when the door was opened gently and the consultant told him that everything had gone well, but that Jane would have to be monitored for the next forty-eight hours by a specialist nurse armed with wire cutters for a speedy intervention in case Jane started to vomit. John shook the surgeon's hand and thanked him profusely.

The next two days were fraught, and Jane was very uncomfortable. She kept crying and kept saying she wished she'd died. Her father and the nurses tried to console her, and said what a lucky escape she'd had, and that she would be as good as new in a few months' time, but it was becoming obvious that Jane's life would never be the same again. It would be a far cry from the seemingly carefree existence she had lived for the past twenty-four years.

***

For the following six weeks, everything Jane ingested had to be liquidised. The nurses were very kind to her and even managed to include her chocolate 'fix' by melting down Mars bars.

As she began the lengthy healing process, she allowed more of her friends to visit, and John felt surplus to requirements, so he visited less often and rekindled his decades-long relationship with the whisky bottle. Elizabeth was too far gone to show any maternal concern for her daughter, and their coexistence was even more fraught as Elizabeth's jealousy of Jane spewed forth in venomous outbursts, including mocking her husband's obvious affection for his eldest daughter whenever he brought her into the conversation.

John would try to do some work up in his office, then he would pop to the golf club and two or three times a week he would visit Jane. On a couple of occasions he took Penny with him, but Jane wasn't very keen on seeing her sister. After several weeks the hospital said she would be well enough to be discharged the following weekend but that she couldn't live alone as she needed extensive physiotherapy. John insisted that Jane was to stay at the 'family home'. This filled her with dread, but she wasn't in a position to argue.

When she was discharged, the nurses bade her a fond farewell. She was a fighter and they had great admiration for her.

She hobbled out to the car with the aid of a walking stick. She was praying that this was a temporary measure and that the physio would enable her to ditch it. She felt like an old lady. Sod that!

On Jane's arrival at the house, her mother barely looked at her. She muttered 'Hello' and scurried off back into her bedroom.

Jane was given Grandma's old room as there was only one flight of stairs for her to negotiate, and it was next to the loo.

As she got herself ready for bed, she could hear her mother goading her father downstairs in the lounge. Jane cringed and nipped to the bathroom in order to avoid her. She then undressed and put in some earplugs, which she had found rather useful in hospital.

She must have managed to doze off eventually because she was woken at some ridiculous hour by Elizabeth sobbing. How could anyone cry that much? 'Christ, just shut up will you,' she muttered through clenched teeth. She had her first physio appointment in the morning. She couldn't wait to be strong enough to escape from this hellhole and get back to her own little sanctuary. She took another couple of painkillers and managed to fall asleep again for a couple of hours.

***

John knocked gently on his daughter's bedroom door and asked if she would like a cup of tea. It was about 8.30 a.m. and Jane really would have preferred to go down to the kitchen to decontaminate all of the utensils. However, she wasn't really up to it, so she said 'Yes please' and suggested he use a cup and saucer, hoping that they might be cleaner.

He reappeared with the tea, and she only found one cat hair on the saucer, which was something of a relief.

She started getting ready for her appointment, and as

she was styling her hair she was rather taken aback when her mother appeared in the doorway. She looked dreadful. Jane looked up warily, waiting for Elizabeth to start on her and was amazed when she merely said, 'I thought I would see how you were feeling today.' Blimey, she sounded as though she actually cared!

Jane smiled and said, 'Thank you for asking. As well as can be expected, considering,' indicating her walking stick.

'Yes, dear, that must be very difficult for you. Hopefully things will improve.' Then she excused herself and disappeared into the bathroom.

Crikey, Jane thought. *That's the nicest she's been to me in years. I wonder how long that will last.*

Her father drove her to her physiotherapy session. Luckily it wasn't far, as his already appalling driving was getting even worse. He was the only person she knew who accelerated when going round corners, sometimes even mounting the kerb (much to the alarm of some poor unsuspecting pedestrian) and then slowed down on the straight. Dear God, she'd only just survived a car crash and she was putting her life at risk by being a passenger in her father's car!

When she returned from the appointment, she was a bag of nerves. She hobbled up the stairs to her room with a cup of tea and took some more painkillers before having a rest. She was seeing a friend later in the day, but she was feeling drained and the medication made her drowsy. Sharon arrived at 5 p.m. and tooted her horn, as instructed by Jane, who had told her not to come to the door. As she made her way down the stairs, she told her father that she would be back in the morning and made her escape before waiting to hear his reply.

Sharon would have loved to go out for a drink but knew that Jane wasn't well enough, and so she settled for a night in with a takeaway and a bottle of wine. Jane didn't touch either. She had brought her knitting and she had some fruit and salad to nibble on. Her jaw was still healing, so chewing was a bit of a problem.

The girls discussed Jane's recovery plan; Sharon had a couple of useful suggestions. Jane always needed a plan, a set of goals. The first was to walk without a stick, the second was to join a gym and try to build up her wasted leg muscles, and the third was to get herself another car, probably an automatic this time.

After a productive night, Sharon went to bed with a fit of tipsy giggles, and Jane slept on the bed settee in the lounge, which was very comfortable, especially as she didn't need her usual earplugs. She managed to get the best night's sleep since before her car crash.

The girls were both up early, as Sharon had to go to work, and so she dropped Jane back at the family home, promising that she would 'rescue' her again later in the week. Jane couldn't wait. She hobbled up the drive to the front door, dreading putting her key in the lock, unsure how much more of her parents' domestic hell she could endure.

***

Jane's physiotherapy sessions were paying off and after six appointments she was advised to join a gym, but to be sensible. She was using her walking stick less and less now and had decided she needed to get back to her flat and some much-needed peace and quiet.

Her father wasn't keen on her leaving, but he couldn't stop her, nor did he blame her. With Elizabeth being the way she was, why would anyone want to stay in this house? He had enjoyed having her home. They shared the same sharp wit and it had been nice to sit watching television with someone who he could engage with. They'd even played chess a few times, which he had loved. He hadn't even minded being beaten. Jane was a clever girl and he was proud of her.

Sharon collected Jane to take her back to her flat. John watched as the car disappeared round the corner and then he took his tumbler of whisky and the rest of the bottle and went and sat in his library, seeking solace in both to fill the void that engulfed his soul.

He passed out in the armchair and was awoken by Skinner scratching at the door to be let in. He staggered to his feet and managed, with the cat in tow, to make his way up to his bedroom on the top floor without disturbing Elizabeth. He then fell asleep with Skinner in his arms. Everyone needed a little comfort once in a while.

**

Over the next few months Jane continued to make progress. She no longer needed the walking stick, was a regular at the local gym, and had been doing some photographic work as she needed to update her portfolio.

To the outside world she had made a miraculous recovery, and everyone kept reminding her of how lucky she had been to survive her car crash practically unscathed. She knew there was no point in trying to explain the physical and emotional pain that she went through on a daily basis.

When she'd had her jaw wired up and her arm and leg in plaster people were extremely sympathetic. However, now she had no outward signs of the trauma that she would have to endure for the rest of her life their concern had worn off. She took strong painkillers religiously, which took the edge off her physical pain, but nothing was ever going to make her whole again. She'd had all the plastic surgery and now she had a wonky chin, and her arm hadn't been set properly so that was skew-whiff. Oh, and she had a limp, which of course threw her back out. Who would want her now? It was a constant battle with dieting, which of course was her way of punishing herself because she loathed her shortcomings so much, and trying to cope with chronic pain.

She had a few good friends, but none of them really knew her. The truth was that she had shut down many years ago, when she realised that she couldn't cope with the reality of her parents' carnage of a marriage. She'd been acting ever since.

One of the drugs she had to take was a muscle relaxant, but it also made her less guarded, less vigilant. She felt very vulnerable. She just wanted someone to look after her, to take her in their arms and say, 'I think you are wonderful just the way you are, I love you and will take care of you forever' – but wearing her heart on her sleeve made her easy pickings for predators. She became a magnet for the wrong sort of person. This highly intelligent, attractive girl who had been such an astute businesswoman was to become the target of some of the most unscrupulous and callous men.

Chapter Twelve

———

Elizabeth had stopped drinking. John couldn't quite believe it and so he marked the vodka bottle that she hid in the laundry basket in the bathroom. This development should have been a reason to celebrate, but her behaviour had taken a dramatic turn for the worse.

She'd started crawling around instead of walking. She would repeat the same thing from the moment she got up to the moment she went to bed, lit numerous cigarettes and left them to burn and had the heating on all day while wearing multiple layers. And it wasn't even autumn yet.

John didn't know what to do, so he asked his younger daughter if she could 'man the phone' and look after her mother.

Penny wasn't working, but she was doing a home course in nutrition, so she would bring her books with her and try to be patient with Elizabeth, but it really was a lot to expect of a young girl with very obvious mental health issues.

She had been seeing a psychiatrist for her eating disorder and suggested to her father that maybe he could help diagnose her mother. John wasn't keen. He didn't like outsiders getting involved in his private life, but as Elizabeth continued to deteriorate, John felt that he had no choice and agreed to a domiciliary visit.

Elizabeth was diagnosed with Korsakoff syndrome, caused by her alcoholism. Her brain had been saturated and her neurological problems were due to being starved of good nutrition, particularly B vitamins, for so many years.

So, at fifty-eight years old, the woman who had been a trailblazer for all the music in Northamptonshire couldn't even remember that she played the piano.

Penny tried her best each day. She cooked Elizabeth some lunch (which she later found had been scraped into a shopping bag) and tried to block out the constant muttering and upsetting repetitious behaviour.

One day after she had escaped back to her bedsit, her father rang to say that her mother had managed to set fire to the bed and the fire brigade had been called. Much against John's wishes, it had been thought best that Elizabeth should be placed in a psychiatric unit for the safety of herself and others.

John's shame hit an all-time high. He retreated to his library in the smoke-filled house, opened a couple of windows, poured himself several large whiskies and wept. How could it have come to this?

It took three days for him to summon up the courage to visit his wife in the institution, but when he caught sight of her queuing up for her hourly rations of cigarettes he couldn't cope, and he fled the scene without her even knowing he had been there. It was like an episode of *Prisoner: Cell Block H*.

John rang Penny and asked if she could go and visit her mother. In the meantime he'd been in touch with a care home, who said that they could possibly offer Elizabeth a private room once she'd stabilised.

The prospect of being able to 'save' his wife and do his 'duty' assuaged his guilt somewhat, and so it was decided that the care home would take Elizabeth for a trial period, along with her beloved (and recently much-neglected) grand piano as an inducement, as one of the owners of the home was a pianist. A week later she was released from the institution and moved into the home. She was the youngest resident by about twenty-five years.

John realised that he wouldn't have enough money to pay the exorbitant care home fees as well as the mortgage repayments on the house, and so he decided to downsize. He'd never much cared for this six-bedroom semi-detached house, and it certainly didn't hold any happy memories. Unfortunately it was absolutely filthy and so John, with his usual dislike of outsiders getting involved, asked Penny if she could help to clean it up a bit, ready for an old friend from the estate agency to do a valuation on it.

Penny spent an entire day trying to make inroads into the filth in the kitchen and needed at least another week of scrubbing to make the rest of the house in the least bit presentable, but her father jumped the gun somewhat and the estate agent turned up prematurely.

Penny was mortified when her father introduced her and proudly announced that she had been tidying up ready for the valuation. John had of course had his usual quota of his favourite beverage and proceeded to offer Frank a drink, which he graciously declined.

Penny didn't dare to look at Frank's expression as her father showed him around the rest of the house. He didn't linger, but they agreed a figure and the next day the board went up.

Chapter Thirteen

Jane had landed herself her dream job. She had been chosen, along with four other girls, to travel to Ireland and then around Europe selling incredibly expensive yachts to wealthy businessmen. The girls travelled by ferry to Ireland, where they were met by a very charismatic self-made multi-millionaire going by the name of Declan O'Leary, who escorted them to their hotel and told them that they would start work first thing the following morning. The girls had a pleasant evening enjoying a few drinks, and Jane mingled for a while but made her excuses as her leg was really hurting. She didn't want to miss out on this golden opportunity, so she needed to get some sleep so she could be on top form for the early-morning briefing.

The following day Declan arrived with his PA, and the girls were all issued with beautiful glossy brochures of yachts that were being constructed locally, in Bray. He wanted the girls to travel to Turkey with him to make a promotional video.

Declan was in his late thirties. He was stocky with wavy brown hair and twinkly blue eyes. The other girls were all vying for his attention, but he seemed to have taken a shine to Jane.

After the briefing, Janette the PA disappeared for the afternoon, so Declan made a beeline for Jane and asked her to join him in his apartment for a drink. Jane was only too keen to get in the boss's good books and so she threw caution to the wind and accepted.

She declined any alcoholic drink, and when Declan inquired as to why she didn't drink, she made a brief reference to her car crash and the painkillers that she had to take. She was surprised that he seemed genuinely interested in her as a person rather than simply trying to get in her knickers, so she let her guard down slightly and mentioned more about her background than she would normally.

The afternoon flew by and finally Declan said that he was so impressed with her that he thought that the pair of them should travel to France together, leaving the others to follow on later with Janette. He told Jane that she was just the type of girl who he thought could go to the very top of the organisation. He then gave her a peck on the cheek and told her to go and get herself something to eat, study the brochures and be ready to leave with him at a moment's notice. He also said he thought it best to keep their arrangement between themselves. It was to be their 'little secret'. With that, he turned on his heel and disappeared, leaving Jane floating on air. She felt like pinching herself. Surely this was too good to be true.

Two days later he picked her up in a taxi and whisked her off to the waiting ferry, on which he had booked a luxury cabin for their fifteen-hour crossing. Jane was so excited, but she tried to contain herself and be professional. After all, it was still just a business relationship – wasn't it?

They spent some time on deck, and then Declan insisted that they have an evening meal. Jane merely picked at hers, and if Declan noticed, he chose not to mention it. He was enjoying a few glasses of wine with his food and regaling her with tales of his businesses and his travels, and how wonderful everything was going to be once they'd made the videos and sold a few more yachts.

Declan then decided that he needed a nap before docking in France. They had about another five hours to go. Jane was surprised to see that it was nearly 1 a.m., and she herself needed some sleep. There was only one bed in the cabin and Declan got undressed and clambered in while Jane showered and cleaned her teeth. When she returned to the cabin, she found him sprawled out, legs akimbo, snoring his head off! She had no intention of sleeping in the chair, so she gave him a shove and he rolled over, freeing up some bed space and some covers. Jane set her alarm; she wanted to be showered and dressed ready for the next leg of their journey before her boss awoke.

Jane watched the port of Roscoff getting closer and closer. Declan joined her and slipped his arm around her tiny waist and apologised for falling asleep and said that hopefully he could make it up to her. She smiled and just tried to enjoy the moment, although she couldn't help wondering what he had meant.

Declan had hired a luxury sports car for their drive through France, and they took in some beautiful sights on their first day on the road and stopped off at a nice hotel to have a meal and get some sleep. They chatted happily about their day over a coffee and then went up to their room. Again, there was only a large double bed, so Jane used the bathroom and was surprised to see Declan was still awake when she had finished her shower. She got into bed beside him, and it seemed he was feeling rather amorous. He started to kiss and caress her, running his fingers gently along her body. She had just begun to relax a little when he guided her head down to his groin while continuing to stroke her back. She licked and sucked, and a few thrusts and a groan later it was all over. He held her for a few moments and then started snoring softly.

Jane silently slid out of bed and sought sanctuary in the bathroom. She felt used, like a whore. Why were men so bloody selfish? She thought that he really liked her. She felt cheap. She cleaned her teeth repeatedly, trying to rid herself of the taste of him, while frantically wiping away hot tears that were running down her face. She splashed cold water over herself and sat on the loo trying to calm down. Had she been deluding herself that he could fancy her. Maybe if she lost some more weight he might find her more attractive. A stricter diet was what was needed, she decided, and she took a couple of painkillers before returning to the bedroom. She got back into bed and eventually managed to fall asleep.

She woke early. It was already getting light and she realised that she was alone. She began to panic. Where was Declan? She looked around the room and couldn't see her handbag. She opened the curtains and realised that the car had gone.

She ran down to reception and was told that monsieur had left about an hour ago. He hadn't paid the bill. Jane was in shock; she couldn't stop shaking. Declan had dumped her and done a runner.

The hotel manager was very kind to her and helped her contact the British Embassy, Scotland Yard and a newspaper who in return for her story would bring her home.

Jane found out that Declan was a con man. He was known to the police and wanted in connection with a number of crimes.

After an exhausting journey back to her hometown, she called in on her father. He, of course, was roaring drunk, and her sister was there, as was Jane's old friend, Sally. Jane didn't want an audience to witness her humiliation, and when her father gave her a very uncomfortable and uncomforting drunken hug and asked if she had anything to help her sleep, it seemed to her that maybe that would be best for everyone. A long sleep and never to wake up.

When she got back to the flat, she got undressed and took an overdose of sleeping pills.

***

Jane came round from a deep sleep with a banging headache and staggered out of bed as she needed the bathroom. She was violently sick and was sitting on the loo with the room spinning when she heard her front door being opened and her sister calling her name. Oh bugger! What did she want?

She was beginning to feel a bit guilty about taking all those pills and would have preferred to have kept quiet about it, but unfortunately she had several missed calls and three voicemails, two from her father (who had sent Penny round) and one from a journalist from a local paper, who she apparently had promised an interview to. She had no recollection of that. She got Penny to ring them and cancel and then she was back in business mode, even though she still felt a little groggy.

Next she had to sort her finances out after having been ripped off by Declan. Penny was in the way; she was really neither use nor ornament at times like this. Jane said she was fine on her own and there had just been a mix-up with her medication, but John instructed his younger daughter to stay with her sister to keep an eye on her. Jane busied herself with paperwork and made a few phone calls regarding her stolen credit cards, and as the day went on she began to feel a little better both physically and emotionally. She sent Penny out to get some food from the corner shop and when she returned Jane made the pair of them an evening meal which consisted mostly of vegetables as Penny was a vegetarian.

After they had finished, they did the washing up together and watched some TV. Jane started knitting frenetically; she found it both therapeutic and constructive, plus she hated being idle. The sooner she could convince her sister and her father that she was safe to be left on her own the better. She was still reeling from the events of the past few days and needed to find a project to try and replenish her dwindling funds and boost her shattered ego.

That night, Penny slept on the bed settee in the lounge and Jane spent half of the night purging herself in the bathroom. Neither of them got much sleep.

The following day John called round to see how Jane was coping and told Penny to stay at least one more night. He thought his eldest child seemed in better spirits and he'd had news that Scotland Yard were hot on Declan O'Leary's heels now, so things were moving in a more positive direction.

John really didn't understand how his daughter managed to get involved with these 'wide boys'. She'd been given a good education, the best of everything really. Why couldn't she find herself a respectable boyfriend?

John didn't stay long because he had to call in at the care home to check on Elizabeth, and then he would go home and read a book with Skinner and several tumblers of whisky for company. He usually fell asleep in his chair and would wake in the early hours and wearily make his way up to his bedroom at the top of the house, closely followed by the cat.

A buyer for the house materialised before long, and John set about trying to find alternative accommodation. He'd decided that he could manage with a decent-sized apartment. He found somewhere suitable fairly quickly and it was just around the corner from Jane's flat, so he could keep an eye on her.

Elizabeth was showing signs of improvement, much to everyone's surprise given her diagnosis. She was regaining her mobility, her memory had improved and she was able to hold some sort of conversation with people again. Harriet, a lady who worked at the care home, offered to take Elizabeth in as she was still not able to live independently but didn't need the care home any more. Harriet's offer was a Godsend, and Elizabeth was quite happy to be a paying guest in her large and comfortable house opposite a park. Penny visited her mother once or twice a week. Jane went less often but their relationship had improved slightly.

Elizabeth seemed to make giant strides in her recovery while staying with Harriet. It transpired that while in the hospital she had been given booster shots of B vitamins and it seemed these had done a remarkable job in restoring Elizabeth's faculties.

The hospital psychiatrist made a follow-up domiciliary visit and had good news: Elizabeth was now fully compos mentis and capable of managing her own affairs again. The first thing she did was to file for divorce from John. It was undeniably something she should have done years before.

However, John couldn't possibly allow a divorce to happen. What would people think? He was now the chairman of the local conservative club and beginning to enjoy his elevated status. He didn't want any scandal jeopardising that.

Over the next few months it became obvious that Elizabeth had made such a good recovery that she really needed her own place. It just so happened that there was a one-bedroom flat for sale in the adjacent block to John's, so he bought it for her. It was a rather odd arrangement but, again, at least he was doing his duty, and they were still married, so he couldn't abandon her if he wanted to. So, Elizabeth and her grand piano were duly installed in a flat that overlooked the flat of her husband, or ex-husband as she had started to call him.

The windows had to be taken out in order to get the piano up and into her flat as there was no way it could be carried up the stairs. Elizabeth never played it, and when Penny visited her with the exciting news that she'd been doing some recording again after quite a long break from singing, her mother showed no interest.

She may have recovered superficially, but the children would never regain the mother they lost all those years ago.

Chapter Fourteen

———

Jane had been very wary of men since her disastrous involvement with Declan, but recently she had been introduced to someone whom she couldn't help but find rather appealing. She decided to take things slowly, and he seemed quite happy to take her out to restaurants and make a fuss of her.

He was a budding film maker and very ambitious. That was something that she admired in a man; she had no time for nine-to-fivers.

One night, when they had been out to a club, Jane invited Andrew in for a coffee. He asked her whether she'd like to watch the trailer to his forthcoming 'blockbuster', and so they snuggled up on the settee and Andrew pointed out various parts of the film that he was proudest of. Jane felt a tiny flicker of interest when he mentioned he was looking for investors but decided to err on the side of caution for the time being.

That night they had sex for the first time. Jane had never had a particularly high sex drive and wasn't very interested, but he was a considerate lover and she felt cared for, which was something she yearned for, probably more than anything else. Andrew was beginning to get under her skin, and she didn't mind at all.

Andrew and Jane had set up a limited company together and now Jane was busy getting investors while Andrew spent a lot of his time filming abroad. When she asked if she could join him on location he always came up with some excuse or other and she was beginning to get the distinct feeling that she was being used. He was living the high life on the money that she had managed to borrow, while she was stuck on her own in boring old Northamptonshire. She had no intention of just sitting at home like some middle-aged married woman, so she started venturing out to nightclubs again with a couple of girlfriends, and it wasn't long before she had another admirer.

Peter, like most of the men that she attracted, was wholly unsuitable. He was married but separated, and within days of them meeting he had the key to her flat and had made himself very much at home. Jane quite enjoyed having a man to fuss over; she was extremely domesticated and quite old-fashioned in some respects.

When Andrew heard about Jane's new suitor, he didn't seem in the least bit bothered. Jane felt very hurt by his indifference but she wasn't going to let him know that – although with her anorexia spiralling out of control it was evident to anyone with eyes in their head that this young lady wasn't coping.

Peter was toying with the idea of moving abroad and quite casually asked Jane if she fancied going with him. She could definitely do with a holiday and the prospect of some sunshine was very appealing, so she said 'Okay, why not?' and within a few days the villa was booked, along with their flights. Jane had given Penny the key to her flat and asked her to keep an eye on the correspondence regarding the film company (as she had received a couple of worrying letters regarding business loans) and Andrew of course had gone AWOL again. Bloody man! Jane told Penny that she would call her when they arrived in Spain and that she planned on travelling back and forth.

Penny seemed a bit subdued at the prospect of her sister leaving and Jane felt she had to reassure her that she wasn't abandoning her. She would be back; she just didn't know quite when.

***

Jane was enjoying this new chapter in her life. She had no idea how long it would last so she was making the most of it.

The villa was gorgeous with a sea view and its own pool, and it was 32°C every day. Not only was she getting a great tan but the pain in her leg had reduced dramatically. The hospital had told her that a warm climate would be beneficial, and it did indeed seem that the sun had great healing properties. Maybe she should consider moving abroad permanently.

Peter was a bit of a boozer and a ten-second wonder between the sheets, but he was paying for everything and looking after her, so although he would certainly never be the love of her life she was content enough, for now.

She joined a local gym and made a few friends and even cut down on her laxative use. Although she didn't eat normally, her eating had become less chaotic as she relaxed into her new surroundings.

They had been in Spain for a couple of months when a phone call from Penny threw her into a state of angst. Penny said she 'didn't really understand why, but the letters said that the banks were going to foreclose on the company's loans'.

Andrew was swanning around Israel with his film crew and was uncontactable. Peter told Jane not to worry, but she couldn't just lay in the sun and do nothing.

She'd even got her mother involved in the film production as an investor. Oh God, what had she done? She knew she had no choice but to return to the UK and try and salvage something, anything, otherwise she could end up in court, or worse. It was decided that Peter would stay in Spain and hopefully Jane would return once she'd sorted everything out.

As she boarded her flight back to England, she knew without a shadow of a doubt that Andrew had fleeced her, and with her name on all the paperwork the banks would be gunning for her. She had no one to blame but herself. She should never have mixed business with pleasure and now she had to face the consequences, alone, and she was petrified.

When she landed at Luton airport, she half expected

to get arrested as she was going through passport control.

She was so exhausted, both physically and emotionally, that when she did eventually arrive home she didn't bother to unpack, just used her spare toothbrush to clean her teeth, removed her make-up, grabbed her winter duvet from the airing cupboard and got straight into bed. She couldn't deal with anything else, she just needed to sleep. The pain in her leg was bad due to the change of climate and so she took a couple of painkillers, and they did the trick. Within half an hour of arriving home, she was spark out.

***

Jane woke with a start. Where was she? Then she realised, and she felt a sinking feeling in the pit of her stomach. She went and had a shower and then decided to have a sunbed session as she was feeling cold – that would help to set her up for what she had to deal with today. Thirty minutes later she got dressed, did her hair and make-up and finished unpacking. She was avoiding the inevitable, which was the pile of letters that Penny had left on her table in the lounge. She wasn't answering her phone either. She'd pulled it out of its socket when she went to bed and had given Peter and her sister strict instructions to ring three times, hang up and ring again, and only then would she answer.

When the flat was tidy and she had finished putting all her clothes either in the washing machine or in the wardrobes, she plugged the phone back in and started to open her letters. By the time she'd read the third demand, she was physically shaking. She was up to her neck in debt. She had borrowed a large amount of money on behalf of Andrew's film company and he hadn't come up with the goods, so they wanted their money back, with interest. She wished she'd stayed in Spain.

She was going to have to speak to her mother and try to explain what had happened. She felt so guilty. Against the odds, she and Elizabeth had formed some sort of relationship after all those years of abandonment. She tried to calm herself down, had a cup of tea (but no breakfast; she couldn't face food) and decided to ring Elizabeth to see what kind of mood she was in.

The phone was answered by Gerard, her mother's very camp cleaner. 'Oh yes, Jane, I'll just put your mummy on.' Elizabeth seemed okay and didn't ask about the film, or Andrew, so Jane said she might pop round to see her as she was just back from Spain.

'Oh, are you, dear? I didn't know you'd been away. Yes, do call round.' And then Elizabeth hung up. She was very vague these days! Oh well, maybe in the circumstances that wasn't a bad thing.

When Jane arrived, she was relieved to see that her father's car wasn't in his garage; she didn't really want to have to explain her situation to him, not just yet. She rang her mother's doorbell and Gerard answered with his Marigold gloves on. He complimented her on her tan and then disappeared back to the kitchen, no doubt to eavesdrop on their conversation. Jane had got the measure of him.

She gave Elizabeth a peck on her overly powdered cheek and said 'yes please' when she was offered a cup of tea, which Gerard dutifully brought through for them on a tray with some biscuits. He then lingered, as if expecting to be asked to join them, but Elizabeth dismissed him in her usual fashion, and he scurried back to his chores. Mother and daughter then talked about the weather, what Elizabeth had been watching on the television and her father's latest girlfriend, who apparently was much older than John and always half-cut. Jane had to smile at this; talk about the pot calling the kettle black!

She looked at her mother, recalling what a stunningly attractive woman she had been. Now her looks were ruined by her smoking and alcoholism, and she looked older than her sixty-one years, even though she had started to make more of an effort and always had her hair dyed and styled. The flat was thick with cigarette smoke and Jane asked if she might open a window ever so slightly.

Elizabeth said, 'Okay, just for five minutes,' as she felt the cold terribly.

Jane didn't really want to bring up her financial problems while Gerard was there, plus she thought her mother looked a little under the weather. As she hadn't mentioned Andrew, Jane decided to delay being the bearer of such bad news for another few days. She said goodbye to her mother and Gerard and said she would come back in a day or so. Her mother, by this time, was watching some quiz programme that she liked and didn't really notice she'd gone. Oh well! She'd go back to the flat and ring her sister.

As she was driving out of the car park, she nearly collided with her father, who was mounting the kerb in his Alfa Romeo. He'd obviously been at the golf club and he had a lady friend in the passenger seat. Crikey, Jane thought. Her mother had been right; she was ancient! She put her hand up to acknowledge him, but he seemed oblivious, so she beat a hasty retreat and drove home with the window wide open to try and get some fresh air after having sat in Elizabeth's smoke-filled flat.

She rang her sister and asked her to come round as she needed someone to discuss this fiasco that she had landed herself in with and sort out an exit plan. Once Penny had arrived, Jane spent most of her time on the phone trying to get hold of Andrew. Penny felt a bit like a spare part and didn't really understand how her incredibly clever sister could get duped by these scumbags; it wasn't even as though they were good-looking or anything!

Finally, Jane managed to contact Andrew's sister, who said that Andrew had written to the banks saying that there had been a few blips in the schedule but that they were trying to recast the lead role and then everything would be back on track, and not to panic. Jane didn't feel particularly reassured by this, as she'd heard it all before, hence trying to make a new life for herself with

Peter in Spain, but she needed to leave England with her business credentials intact, not in tatters.

The girls sat and chatted about their mother and the awful woman their father had taken up with. She drank even more than he did! Penny had seen her a few times while visiting her mother, which she did several times a week.

Jane described the villa in Spain and invited Penny to visit. She wished her little sister was a bit more sociable; she had become very insular. Jane asked her if she could pop round again in a couple of days, as she may have got further with sorting out the banks. Penny said, 'Yes okay, just ring me,' and disappeared back to her flat, leaving her sister to a restless night, worrying about where it would all end.

***

Jane spent the next few days talking to banks, trying to reassure them that the filming would resume very soon and begging them to give the company just a little more time, but they'd had enough of being fobbed off, so she decided it was time to seek legal advice. As she was practically destitute, thanks to Andrew, she decided to call in at the Citizens Advice Bureau in the town. She rang Penny as she didn't fancy having to sit around waiting on her own but got no reply. She tried a couple more times (just in case she was in the loo), but still no answer. Maybe she had gone round to their mother's flat; Penny did spend a lot of time with her. Jane decided she would pop round and see if she could see her sister's car and take it from there.

As she pulled into the car park, she was horrified to see her mother on a stretcher being put into an ambulance, which was surrounded by a group of people. Jane pushed through frantically, trying to catch a glimpse of Elizabeth but it was too late; the paramedics shut the doors and sped off with the sirens going. She saw Penny, who was crying inconsolably. Jane couldn't really get any sense out of her – something about the police having to break in and finding Elizabeth unconscious on the lounge floor. Jane felt sick, but she knew that she had to take charge. Penny went back to the 'safety' of her mother's flat, and Jane said that she would meet her at the hospital.

Penny tried to pull herself together and repair her make-up but failed on both counts as the tears kept falling. She eventually made her way to the hospital, where her sister was standing by Elizabeth's bed. Their mother was hooked up to a monitor, and Penny went and sat by her bed and held her hand. Jane was talking to the staff nurse about Elizabeth's condition when suddenly the monitor stopped beeping. The girls were quickly ushered out of the ward and taken to a side room. Jane was ashen and wished her sister would stop bloody crying, but she kept that thought to herself. After what seemed like an eternity, the nurse came and told the girls that she was very sorry, but Elizabeth had passed away, and there had been nothing anybody could have done to save her. The nurse reassured them that she wouldn't have been in any pain.

The two girls were in shock. They were both only in their twenties, and although Elizabeth had been emotionally unavailable to them since they were children she had recently begun to show signs of her old self. Before the heartache, alcohol and resulting chaos she had been a loving mother. How could this be happening? It was so unfair.

They made their way back to their mother's flat, both in turmoil, but Jane internalised her feelings while Penny's surged out. As they walked across the flat's car park they saw their father standing with his head bowed; he looked as though he had the weight of the world on his shoulders. When he saw his daughters approaching, he became more upright and started talking in a most business-like fashion with his eldest child. He, like Jane, couldn't handle Penny's weeping and had no words of comfort for her.

Penny felt like screaming. All she wanted was a hug, someone to say something reassuring. For God's sake, their mother had just died and they still couldn't connect.

They all went back to their respective homes. Penny was greeted by her latest boyfriend, who tried his best to console her.

Jane returned to her flat still unable to shed a tear and gorged herself on ice cream and chocolate, washed down with a packet of laxatives. The self-loathing at having betrayed Elizabeth by involving her in Andrew's company combined with feelings of deep remorse and incredible sadness for all the wasted years, and a wave of despair engulfed her. She spent most of the night purging, and eventually she started to cry.

John sat in his flat with Skinner on his lap and a bottle of whisky by his side. He didn't want to feel anything. Elizabeth had been the closest thing he had ever known to love. It was such an alien concept to him. He could only really show it with his pets.

He stood up and walked over to the window and stared at his wife's flat in sheer disbelief that he would never see her again. They'd been to hell and back and it was his fault – he knew that. Guilty as charged.

As he gulped down another tumbler of anaesthetic, he felt tears burning behind his eyes, threatening to burst forth. When he could hold them back no longer, he let out a cry that sounded like it came from a wounded animal and sank to the floor in a crumpled heap. He stayed that way for some time, until the cat came over meowing and John managed to get to his feet and made his way to the bedroom, where he passed out on his bed, fully clothed.

Chapter Fifteen

Elizabeth was cremated. There were only seven people at the service. It was as though John couldn't bear to be judged as the failure he knew himself to have been as a husband, so he kept the funeral very low-key.

There was no music. The minister said a few words and then poor David (who was an emotional wreck) had to press the button that closed the curtains and carried the coffin to the furnace. Penny fidgeted throughout the service and at one point thought that she might collapse.

The whole place was like a conveyer belt of grief. As one family left, another was waiting outside for their twenty minutes of heartbreak. There was no wake. No celebration of Elizabeth's glory days when she took the town by storm with her music-making. A pitiful send-off for a tragic life, cut short by addiction and heartache.

Jane immediately started organising solicitors and then left for Spain, planning on sorting out some estate agents for her mother's flat upon her return. Elizabeth had left her three children equal shares in its sale, but she'd gifted Penny a little extra as they'd been so close in her final months.

Penny was sleeping at the flat. She couldn't cope with losing her mother; she was absolutely devastated. She felt lost and so alone. Jane returned like a whirlwind, upsetting Penny's equilibrium, which she was clinging onto by her fingertips. Jane had decided that she was emigrating once the sale of the flat went through. She explained to her sister that she'd had enough of trying to deal with the fall-out from Andrew's film company and that she would leave Penny in charge of all the finances. Jane would be giving up her flat, and she asked if she could store suitcases full of clothes and other personal possessions in Penny's ground-floor flat.

Penny didn't really understand why her sister was abandoning her so soon after Elizabeth's death. She wasn't getting on very well with her boyfriend and as she'd spent so much time with her mother she was really lonely. But Jane told her to keep her chin up and said she would only be a plane trip away.

As the will was so straightforward and the property market was booming, Elizabeth's flat sold after only a week on the market. Penny had to move back into her own flat with her moody boyfriend and Jane got on the night flight back to Spain. It was time to try and put all of this angst behind her and start a new life in the sun with Peter.

***

Peter and Jane lived together in the villa for just over six months. Jane continued to go to the gym and became good friends with another English girl, named Lucy. Peter was fifteen years older than Jane; he drank too much and was also a compulsive gambler. They had very little in common. The couple began bickering quite a lot and as usual Jane punished herself by dieting. Peter then began to become abusive towards her, saying he'd wanted a 'trophy girlfriend, not a bag of bones'. That was the beginning of the end.

Lucy could see that her friend wasn't happy. She was also acutely aware that she was suffering from anorexia, and her heart went out to her as her sister had suffered with the same eating disorder. Jane confided in her about Peter's behaviour and Lucy said that she was planning on going to the Greek island of Rhodes to do some seasonal work selling boat trips. It basically consisted of looking glamorous in a bikini, a bit of sales pitch and sunning yourself all day. Jane said it sounded wonderful but dreaded breaking the news to Peter. She needn't have worried: Peter had decided to give up the villa and return to the UK, so they parted relatively amicably.

The two girls were young, free and single, and as they boarded the plane Jane was filled with excitement at the prospect of her new adventure and the chance of actually having some fun – something she hadn't had in a very long time.

They were met at the airport by an old friend of Lucy's. The girls were going to share an apartment on the outskirts of Faliraki, and Lucy's friend Simon had arranged it all for them. Jane suspected that Lucy and Simon had been an item at some point, but she didn't pry; Lucy would tell her if she wanted to.

The apartment, while not overly spacious, was lovely. It had one bedroom and a sofa bed in the lounge, so it gave both girls a place to lay their heads and a bit of privacy if they were 'entertaining'.

Lucy was very attractive. She had long brown hair, almond-shaped green eyes and a figure to die for. Jane's hair had lightened in the sun during her time in Spain, so she had gone the whole hog and bleached it blonde. It really suited her, and the two girls were enjoying a lot of attention from the local men.

They settled into their day job, selling boat trips dressed in very skimpy bikinis and found a local gym to feed both of their exercise addictions. Lucy was relieved to see that Jane had gained a little bit of weight and was beginning to look healthier as well as happier.

Jane wrote regularly to her sister and father. She told Penny that she was really happy, probably for the first time in her life. She decided to learn Greek (well, try to). It was a difficult language, but Jane had found somewhere on the planet where she felt she belonged, and so when the summer season ended she decided to keep the flat on and make Rhodes her permanent home. Lucy, however, was moving back to Spain and wanted to spend some time with her family in England. Jane saw her off at the airport, and as she hugged her friend goodbye she knew how much she would miss her. She had been a true friend and had been there for her in her hour of need. They promised to stay in touch, and Jane knew that they would.

Jane decided to return to England in the colder months, just for a few weeks. She had a friend she could stay with, and if all else failed she could stay at her father's flat. She walked to the local gym and called in at her sister's. She had a mountain of paperwork to deal with but was feeling a lot more secure about her financial position since she'd emigrated. Debt collectors couldn't get blood out of a stone after all, and she, to all intents and purposes, owned absolutely nothing.

She invited her sister to stay the following season, hoping that Penny would become a bit more outgoing. She had only ever been abroad once and that was for one week with her friend from school. They went to Portugal in October, and it rained on two of the days. Typical!

Jane was quite good at living out of suitcases but happily returned to her new home in Rhodes in late February. It was about 16°C and raining but she was pleased to be back. She was a popular girl in the community and she decided to start attending the local Greek Orthodox church services.

She was doing her very best to fit in and embrace everything about this wonderful island, and it seemed to be embracing her right back.

***

Jane was pleased to discover that there was an apartment available for long-term rent right next door to the gym that she used and it was considerably cheaper than the one she had rented with Lucy, so she moved in and soon had it looking just the way she wanted. She continued with her Greek language lessons and spent time at the monastery as she was thinking of being baptised into the Greek Orthodox faith. She had such a deep-seated desire to be accepted, to be 'the good girl' that she had always been as a child, a people-pleaser.

The church criticised her appearance; they disliked her long painted nails and the way she dressed when selling boat trips. What felt even crueller was that she couldn't use her lovely singing voice to its full capacity in church, because singing across more than one octave was forbidden as it had been deemed to be showing off. So when she was invited to anything remotely religious, she would wear respectable clothes and very little make-up, and she never sang.

It was like being two different people. She loved the attention she got from men when she was working on the beach. She even dated a few, but once they'd got into her knickers they didn't hang around for long. She knew that she could be hard work sometimes, but on a good day she thought she was attractive, very feminine, intelligent, good company and good in bed. On a bad day, however (such as when she'd been dumped for no good reason), she was the girl with a limp, who had an eating disorder, no tits, on pain medication for life, a psychological mess. Why would anyone want her?

That summer Jane was rather surprised, but very pleased, to receive a letter from her sister asking if she could visit and bring a male 'friend' with her, and so Jane made arrangements for them to stay at a local hotel. Penny arrived with Steve in tow. Jane didn't take to him and the feeling was mutual, so he spent the week exploring the island on his own.

The girls had a good time. Penny had been to France and Italy already that year and had a good tan, so she was happy to spend her days soaking up the sun with her sister and her friends.

The night they went clubbing would be imprinted on the memories of quite a few of the locals for many years to come. Jane wasn't a dancer; even before her car crash she was a 'dancing round your handbag' type of girl, whereas her sister – well! She had worked in clubs at the tender age of sixteen (having lied about her age, of course). In fact, her ballet teacher had said she'd never seen anyone dance like her and promptly arranged for her to dance at the Anglia TV dinner and dance that year.

So when Donna Summer's 'I Feel Love' came on in the club, Penny – by then a few drinks in – took over the dance floor.

Unfortunately, Greek men had a different reaction to her gyrations, and she ended up with about twenty men all standing around her, offering their drinks to her. She was drenched in sweat and no doubt very thirsty, but Jane shouted, 'Don't accept a drink! They will think they've pulled!' and they had to beat a hasty retreat out of the back door to avoid being mobbed.

Jane thought it was hilarious. 'Trust you to get us into trouble. You'll ruin my reputation if the monastery get to hear about it,' she mock-scolded. Penny had enjoyed herself, and she'd definitely made an impact!

The visit ended too quickly, but Jane would be returning to the UK for a few weeks in November, so they arranged another night out. It was something for them both to look forward to.

***

Jane flew back to England in November; she was going to stay with her friend Neal, who had a flat in the town centre and was always happy to see her.

She had decided on some more cosmetic procedures while she was in the UK and factored in some recovery time before flying back to Rhodes. She was having a lower eye lift and had found a surgeon in Birmingham who came highly recommended. He would also do some liposuction for her. She got a discount for having both of the procedures done at the same clinic. She was convinced that she had terrible cellulite, so when one of her male friends made a flippant comment about her bottom it was the final straw and she felt she had no choice – she had to have some fat removed. Many surgeons would have turned her away, because it was so obvious she had an eating disorder and body dysmorphia, but some were only too happy just to take people's money.

Both procedures went well, and Jane was pleased with the results. She was very sore for a couple of weeks and glad she'd arranged to stay in the UK while she healed.

She stayed in England for Christmas, which was

always a miserable affair. The family never got together. Penny would sometimes pay a 'duty visit' to their father on Christmas Day, but once he'd had a few drinks he always went over the top and was just plain nasty.

This year the two girls spent an hour at his flat with his new girlfriend. This meant that they had to pass their mother's flat, which was very upsetting. During the visit their father consumed most of a bottle of rather expensive and very strong red wine. The sisters were on tenterhooks, waiting for their father's usual tirade of abuse, and when he started they beat a hasty retreat. The girlfriend had just sat there with a glass in her hand and smirked. No wonder they got along so well. Both highly critical of others and emotionally bankrupt.

Penny went home in tears and Jane went back to Neal's and made herself sick. 'Joy to the world' it most certainly was not.

***

After her surgery had healed, Jane spent some time with an old friend and her young children, to whom Jane was godmother. Sue was a straight-talking woman who had lived in the flat next door to Jane before she got married and bought a house. She told Jane that she was way too thin, that she really didn't understand anything about eating disorders but that she was pleased to see her, and that Jane seemed a lot happier living abroad, so at least that had been a positive move. She said she just wished that Jane could meet someone and maybe get married, settle down and even have a baby. She'd soon forget about dieting then! If only it were that straightforward.

Jane returned to Rhodes in the early spring. She had decided that she was going to be baptised into the Greek Orthodox faith. She needed to feel that she belonged. She wanted to feel the way she had felt when she visited her grandparents. She needed to feel that inner glow. She was crying out to be loved.

***

Jane was dressed in a plain white linen robe with a cross on the front. She wore no make-up and her perfectly manicured nails were left unvarnished.

Jane had been having private counselling sessions in preparation for her baptism into the Greek Orthodox faith and they decided that she was now well versed enough for the service to go ahead. She had chosen her godparents and they had taken great care in organising the day for their new godchild. Today was the day.

During the service, which consisted of a lot of chanting and incense-wafting, she was immersed three times in the baptismal font. She was lifted into it by two of the male guests and then wrapped up in another robe to receive her first holy communion.

After the service, they celebrated Jane's special day with a meal and a massive cake. She was very touched and felt a little of the closeness that she had shared with her grandparents.

The Greek Orthodox church was very strict, but Jane

had always believed in God. Obviously she'd not attended church for a few years and she was happy to be able to worship again. Same God, different religion and customs. When she went to bed that night, she didn't feel quite so alone.

***

Jane's life was quite full.

She had her job on the beach, she was going to the gym four or five times a week, still taking her Greek language lessons, and now she was involved with the church. But something was missing and she'd yearned for it all her life: someone to love her unconditionally. She was still young, but some nights, when she was sitting knitting another creation for a friend, she felt about sixty. Sex symbol by day, old spinster by night. She couldn't bear to be bored. Regardless of her injuries, she was still up for an adventure, something to get the blood pumping.

A couple of weeks later it seemed her prayers had been answered (well, on the excitement front anyway). An all-male dance troupe were booked to appear at a local nightclub, and they were also working out at the same gym that Jane used. She was already training when they made their entrance. Most of the women just gawped at them, but Jane was a little more subtle. They were gorgeous but they knew it, and she had no intention of just being another groupie. She continued with her workout and exited the gym without speaking to them, not because she was being antisocial but because she was sure she would see them again at some point during their stay.

Later that afternoon, she was on the beach wearing her white fringed bikini and she realised she was being observed (not very discreetly) by one of the dancers. She smiled and when he approached her, she asked if he wanted to go on a boat trip.

Only if you come with me,' he replied.

He was very good-looking, but she said she couldn't because she was working.

He obviously wasn't used to being turned down and his passing shot hit her right in the crumple button. 'I thought you looked a bit like Pamela Anderson standing there with your windswept blonde hair and legs up to your armpits, but she's got a couple of things that you haven't! If you had tits, you'd be dangerous.' With that, he walked away to join his mates at a nearby bar.

Jane flinched. She felt as though she'd been punched. Her eyes filled with tears, which she frantically tried to stop from falling. She managed to regain some composure and continued with her shift, but that night she went home and binged on ice cream and chocolate and then swallowed a packet of laxatives.

The next day she went to the gym and when the dance troupe came in she, to all intents and purposes, ignored them. The blond one who had inadvertently 'destroyed' her with his remark waved at her and she inclined her head in acknowledgment, because she was well bred.

Jane cut her workout short and decided to go and get ready for her shift on the beach (plus she felt like hell after her night on the loo). She had a quick shower before changing into a lovely yellow swimsuit and tied her blonde hair into a high ponytail. She surveyed her reflection in the full-length mirror and knew that she had no option but to have a boob job. She'd always had a thing about being flat-chested, but she'd worn push-up bras and starved herself so she didn't look so pear-shaped. Maybe the blond dancer had done her a favour and forced her arm. Jane looked again at her reflection, imagining how she would look with size 32C implants. Now the seed was sown there was no turning back.

She daydreamed her way through her shift. Two of her girlfriends asked if she was going to watch the dance troupe at the club that night, as they had a spare ticket. Jane wasn't keen, but they eventually managed to twist her arm, and the trio agreed to meet outside the gym next to her flat.

She made a special effort with her outfit that evening. She wore a sparkly blue crop top and matching netted short skirt. It showed off her tiny waist and her toned, tanned legs. She curled her hair and left it loose, using half a can of hairspray to hold it in place. She looked stunning.

Her two friends arrived and they set off to the club. When they arrived, her friends had had a couple of drinks, but Jane stuck to soft drinks. The place was heaving, mostly with women, and the music was deafening. She was just beginning to wish she'd stayed at home when the show started with a bang! Bloody hell – Jane suddenly realised that they were strippers!

The women were going crazy, and there was baby oil everywhere. They were shoving their toned bottoms in people's faces, and the atmosphere was on fire. After the initial shock, Jane watched them 'work the room' with a detached admiration. Her sister sprang to her mind, and she wondered what she would have made of them. There was one very attractive one with long dark hair who was definitely Penny's type.

When they ripped off their thongs before running offstage, she did actually gasp and then she started laughing. Her friends were salivating, and she was giggling. My God, what a night. She'd just been baptised into a strict religion where the sins of the flesh were, well, just that – SINS – and then this!

As the girls made their way home, Jane decided that she was glad she'd been persuaded to ditch her knitting and go out that night. It had been a real eye-opener, in more ways than one.

The following morning two of the strippers were using the weights next to the pec deck that she was on. She smiled and said, 'I enjoyed your show last night. My sister's a dancer!' They had a chat and said that if ever she was in London to look them up and exchanged numbers.

She saw all four of them later on, each with a starstruck girl in tow, and she managed to sell them all a boat trip. Result!

She saw them a few more times, always with a different collection of girls (which made her so pleased that she hadn't been tempted), but the men were young and good-looking with girls throwing themselves at their feet, so you could hardly blame them,.

They came to say goodbye to her when their two-week contract was up. She gave them each a hug, even the rude blond one, who had the cheek to pinch her bum! No decorum!

She said she'd be in touch when she returned to England later in the year.

It's fair to say the dance troupe had brought a lot of energy to the island that summer. It was a lot less exciting after they left.

Jane went back to her knitting and to planning her next move to becoming 'dangerous'.

***

The boob job was to be done in Athens. Jane had located a highly skilled surgeon and had run his name past a couple of her friends, who had given her the thumbs-up. The recovery time was rather long, so Jane planned to stay with an old friend, Stella, for two weeks post-op and then return to the island. If all went to plan, she would then fly to England for a few weeks when she had fully healed. She was really excited. She was sure that this surgery would make everything perfect – or, to quote a very sexy blond dancer, 'dangerous'. She could not wait!

She didn't tell her sister, or indeed anybody in England, what she had planned. Penny had told her not to keep having surgeries, so she'd definitely disapprove.

In early November she travelled to the mainland and went through with this incredibly risky and painful operation. Stella looked after her wonderfully. Jane healed well and was absolutely blown away with her new look. She'd waited all her life to have breasts and she had now fulfilled her dream. This was it; her life could now begin. Watch out, world!

She returned to Rhodes and kept herself 'under wraps'. The tourist season had finished, so she had several months before the 'unveiling' of her new body on the beach. She told a couple of her Rhodes girlfriends, but still no one in the UK.

A month later she flew to England. She was going to stay at Neal's again. Her flight was late and so she was greeted by a very grumpy Neal, who moaned for the duration of the drive home. She was very fond of him, but he really could be a miserable old git when he wanted to be, and then of course there was the other miserable old git – Daddy dearest, who she would have to pay a duty visit to, and also her sister, who Jane hoped would be feeling a bit more sociable; you could never tell with her. Jane thought about Penny, in her bohemian ground-floor flat that had ivy growing through the bedroom window and a cat flap with no flap, meaning that half the neighbourhood's cats came and went as they pleased. Jane wasn't sure exactly how many cats called Penny's flat home, but she knew that she needed to take a lot of Sellotape round when she visited!

After a reasonable night's sleep at Neal's, Jane walked to the gym. She'd got her thermals on because it was pretty chilly and her injuries really hurt in the cold. Her workout warmed her up a bit and when she'd finished she chatted to some of the bodybuilders she was friendly with. She was aware that some of them took anabolic steroids and wondered if they might be useful to her as she was trying to build her muscles up. The men were only too keen to talk about their regimes and even gave her a few samples with some basic instructions on dosage and their benefits. They also showered her with compliments about how 'hot' she looked, and a couple even asked her out, but she wasn't interested, and said she was too busy, maybe some other time.

She left the gym and called at Penny's on the off-chance that she was in. Penny ushered her to the front room, where Jane spent a good ten minutes de-hairing the bed settee before parking her well-toned bottom on it. She then produced her knitting from her 'Mary Poppins' bag and continued with her latest creation while her sister puffed pensively on a cigarette. Jane chatted away, but she didn't mention her surgery. Over the course of Jane's hour-long visit, several cats wandered into the front room, and one even made an attempt to sit on her lap, but Jane shooed it away with her perfectly manicured hands and luckily it took the hint. She, unlike her sister, wasn't an animal lover. They were way too messy for her. She asked Penny if she fancied going clubbing and was pleasantly surprised when she said that she wouldn't mind.

Jane had an appointment to see her doctor while she was in England. She had been on strong painkillers ever since her car crash and she got various people to collect her prescriptions and post them to her every month, but occasionally she did have to have a medication review in person.

She got on very well with her doctor and during her consultation she did mention that she sometimes felt a little 'down' in the winter months and was immediately prescribed an antidepressant. She was already planning on dabbling in anabolic steroids; what harm could another little pill do?

She started taking her new pills and went on with life, meeting up with a couple of old friends over the next few days. She had been feeling okay, quite pumped up really, brimming with new-found confidence over her curvier shape perhaps, so she was knocked sideways when she was walking back to Neal's flat and her heart started racing and she felt as though she was going to pass out. Luckily she was with Penny, who suspected she was having some kind of panic attack. She had never seen Jane so out of control, so vulnerable, and it scared her. She managed to get hold of a paper bag and eventually Jane started to calm down and stop hyperventilating.

On returning to the flat Jane excused herself and said

she thought she'd best go to bed for a rest, which she did, and Neal gave Penny a lift home. Jane lay on her bed in the middle of the afternoon listening to the hustle and bustle of passers-by and wondered if perhaps she should lower the dose of the steroids she was taking. She would ask the lads at the gym the next day. She didn't fancy a repeat performance of today.

***

Jane returned to Rhodes after having spent over a month in England. Neal drove her to the airport, and as she gave him a quick hug goodbye, she realised that she would miss him. Jane knew that he thought the world of her, so she planted a kiss on his ageing cheek, which obviously pleased him, and he beamed down at her as she wiped her lipstick marks away with a tissue.

It was late February and she had decided that she would use the rest of the winter months to work even harder on her body. She was on a mission. She'd managed to find someone to supply her with steroids and she hoped to have increased her muscle mass by the beginning of the tourist season. She couldn't wait to wear her new bikinis to show off her assets!

Her 'Greek family' were pleased to see her at church on the Sunday. She was touched when they told her that they'd missed her. They were very kind and tried to include her in all of their religious celebrations.

For the next two months she stuck to a very strict regime of diet and exercise. She felt quite pumped up and was really looking forward to the summer. She spent most of her evenings sitting alone in her flat watching the odd English soap opera, letter-writing and knitting jumpers and baby clothes. She had friends who would call by for a chat and a coffee, but she really wished she had a boyfriend to worship the ground she walked on, or at the very least give her a cuddle and tell her everything was going to be alright. She was always fretting over her dwindling finances, and she worried that she might not be able to work if her arthritis worsened with age. It would be lovely to meet a decent man who would take care of her, but she was always attracted to the bad boys, and they to her.

She wrote to her sister telling her she was feeling a bit lonely and asking if maybe she fancied another holiday in Rhodes. A few people had visited over the years, including David's girlfriend, who wasn't really Jane's cup of tea but who had arrived with a suitcase full of Jane's shopping and had a cheap holiday in the sun in return.

The weeks passed, the rain stopped and suddenly blue skies and sunshine returned as if by magic, as they did every year.

The tourist season was beginning, and the island was coming to life. Jane was able to sunbathe on her flat roof, topping up her tan and getting much-needed pain relief.

Within the next two to three weeks, the beaches would get busier, and she would be selling boat trips once again, enticing holidaymakers to part with their hard-earned money, so that she could pay her rent. She was good at her job and was hoping that her new curvier body would get her some much-needed attention.

By the beginning of May the island of Rhodes was buzzing, and Jane was working long hours. She got chatted up on a regular basis and responded with smiles and friendliness but politely declined their advances, basically because they didn't interest her.

And then Steve arrived. Blond, muscular, in his early forties. He was from New Zealand and owned a bungee jumping business. He was staying for the season. Within a week of his arrival he seemed to have acquired some 'groupies', but he took all of this in his stride; he had set his sights on Jane, and he was used to getting what he wanted.

***

Steve and Jane started off as friends, but Steve was a fast worker and so within a week he'd moved into Jane's flat. As they were sleeping together it sort of made sense and saved Steve having to pay for his own accommodation. He was a charmer and a chancer, but Jane was enamoured of him and accepted him warts and all. He made a fuss of her, and she finally was living her dream of having someone to cuddle up with after a long day at work.

Without a doubt, Steve had landed on his feet. Jane was good-looking, intelligent and she was a domestic goddess. He was definitely going to enjoy this summer season. They made an attractive couple, and Jane's friends were pleased that she had found herself a steady boyfriend. The pair were often seen walking hand-in-hand and cuddling in public. Jane confided in Steve about her family, her parents' alcoholism and her chaotic childhood and he seemed quite sympathetic and reassuring. He was also a considerate lover and generally he made her feel special. He was definitely a keeper. She was totally smitten.

They'd been living together for nearly two months when Jane made a fatal mistake. After an exceptionally passionate lovemaking session, she'd snuggled up with him, let her guard down and told him that she loved him. He didn't say it back, just got up and went to the bathroom, got back into bed and went to sleep. Jane lay next to him fretting and unable to relax but eventually she managed to drift off.

When she woke, Steve had gone. She panicked. She couldn't lose him. She threw on a sundress and set off in the direction of his workplace. He must have left early because he had a lot of bookings. She had to see him to make sure that everything was alright between them.

She caught sight of him with a very attractive twenty something busty brunette. Jane felt a twinge of jealousy; was she there for bungee jumping, or was she after Steve? Jane smiled and waved, and Steve did the same, but when she went to give him a hug and a kiss he said, 'Not now, Jane. I'm at work. I'll catch you later.' She felt humiliated, snubbed and rushed back to the flat, brushing away tears of deep-seated pain.

She managed to do her sales pitch on the beach that day, blonde hair in a little topknot, a yellow bikini, perfectly painted nails to match her painted-on smile. When the last boat came back into shore, she hurried back to the flat so that she could shower and get dolled up ready for an evening in with Steve. He came home later than he usually did, and Jane said that supper was ready whenever he was. He replied that he wasn't really hungry and fancied going out for a beer – alone. He told her not to wait up.

She rushed out after him. 'Steve! Steve! We need to talk.'

'Not now, Jane. Just leave it.'

She tried to calm herself down, but she felt that she had lost him, and she couldn't bear it.

She decided to give her sister a quick ring. She'd meant to earlier, but the day hadn't exactly gone to plan. It was Penny's birthday, and she was having problems with her landlord over her tenancy agreement and was worried to death about being evicted. Jane wished her sister happy birthday down the phone. Penny said thanks but sounded really subdued. Jane said that she couldn't stop but not to worry as she had a plan. Penny sounded relieved by this, and then Jane said, 'Must dash. Enjoy your special day' and put the phone down.

She couldn't settle, so she decided to go to the gym for an hour. She took some steroids to see if they would pump her up a bit, and she worked out using slightly heavier weights than normal. She had hoped that the extra exercise would help calm her down, but her nerves were shredded.

She went back to the flat and demolished several bowls of ice cream followed by a large slice of black forest gateau and washed it all down with a glass of Epsom salts. She spent most of the night on the loo and only managed to get a couple of hours' sleep.

She was woken by an extremely drunk and belligerent boyfriend, who'd staggered back to the flat to sleep off his boozy night out. He just made it to the bathroom to throw up but missed the toilet bowl, and then collapsed onto the bed in a drunken heap.

Jane knew better than to antagonise a drunken man, so she let him sleep and went and mopped up his vomit. She then cleaned the rest of the bathroom and when she'd finished she decided to go outside and lay in the sun. She felt terrible after her night of purging, but she put a brush through her hair and made herself look as attractive as possible.

When Steve came round he had a banging head and was in a foul mood. Jane had heard him get up and use the bathroom, so she came in and asked him if he was okay.

That's when Steve flipped. 'Why don't you learn to keep your mouth shut! You're smothering me. I can't breathe. I didn't sign up for anything heavy, just a bit of fun for a few weeks, not some anorexic nutjob with plastic tits.'

Jane recoiled, stunned by his cruelty. Losing all of her usual composure, she burst into floods of tears. Steve gave her a pitying look. 'I'm leaving, Jane. I can't stand any more of this. I'm not a psychiatrist.'

Jane replied, 'If you leave me, I will jump from the roof.'

Steve scoffed at her remark, grabbed his cases, threw all of his belongings in them and stormed out of the flat without a backward glance.

Jane knew that it was pointless trying to reason with him, and she was too upset to even think straight. She crawled into bed and cried her heart out.

She must have nodded off because when she looked at her watch it was almost time for her shift on the beach. She didn't know how she could face going to work. Having studied her puffy face she decided that sunglasses were a must, and she would make an appearance, even if it was just for an hour before crying off sick. At work she was very subdued, not her usual chatty self, and after a couple of hours she told Paolo she didn't feel too good, and he told her to go home and maybe take a couple of days off. She forced a smile and thanked him.

On her way back to the flat she saw her friend Sara. She asked Jane if she was okay. Jane sighed and said that Steve was being horrible and that he'd left her.

Sara said, 'Oh dear. I'm sure he'll be back. You make a great couple.'

Jane replied, 'He said I'm pathetic and was really abusive. I wish that I was dead.'

Sara was shocked and replied, 'Don't say such terrible things. Men can be a pain at times. He'll come round. Take care, Jane. I must rush.'

Jane watched her disappear down the street. No one seemed to want to be around her anymore.

Just as she was approaching her flat she saw Steve, closely followed by the busty brunette she'd seen him with the previous day. If he saw her he didn't acknowledge her, and Jane's heartache was all-consuming. She put her key in the front door and made her way into the bedroom. She had come to a decision.

Chapter Sixteen

The following morning Jane was on autopilot. She got up, showered and dressed. She then took some money that she had in her bedside cabinet and made her way up to Steve's place of work. The young brunette wasn't with him, but he looked ill at ease as he spotted her approaching. She kept it very business-like; in fact she surprised herself at how calm she appeared to be.

'Here's the money I owe you, Steve. Don't worry, I won't bother you again.'

He took the money, unable to meet her gaze, but there was no apology forthcoming.

As Jane turned to leave she said, 'By the way, you have a really cruel streak to your personality. I feel sorry for the next girl that you hook up with. Maybe you would benefit from some counselling or anger management classes.'

She turned and walked away from the man that she loved so much, sunglasses firmly in place as hot tears ran down her pretty face. She stumbled slightly as the path was uneven and her leg was hurting like hell. She passed a couple of her friends and managed to say hello but didn't stop for a chat. She just wanted the world to go away. She was fed up with pretending, living this fake life. Steve had dumped her, basically saying that she was a waste of space. She kept replaying his violent outburst and she felt utterly worthless. All the cosmetic procedures, all the pain, and for what? She had no one. She was totally alone.

Her head was banging, and she was getting more and more stressed. She entered her home and locked the front door behind her, leaving the key in the lock.

Tears of despair poured down her face and she sobbed uncontrollably. She sat on the bed, took her diary out and began writing. She was becoming hysterical and took a handful of pills washed down with water.

She picked up the phone to ring Neal, and she was taken aback when he answered as she was expecting the answerphone. The room started spinning and her speech was slightly slurred. She managed to say, 'I'm sorry for the trouble, but I've taken loads of pills and I won't be around any more. I love you.' She hung up, leaving the phone off the hook.

She tried to take another handful of pills but started choking on them. She was still scribbling things in her diary, but she was fighting a losing battle.

Neal had tried to call her back to no avail, and then he'd rung the British Embassy to get them to send the police round to Jane's flat. An hour or so later they arrived. They tried the front door, but got no answer, so they went away again. Sometime afterwards, two of her friends tried to get into her flat using a spare key, but the key was in the lock on the inside, so they went round to the side and forced the window. They found Jane naked on her living room floor surrounded by broken glass and tablets. One of them checked for a pulse while the other called for an ambulance. The paramedics tried to resuscitate her on the way to the hospital, but there was nothing that they could do to save her, and she was pronounced dead on arrival.

She had written in her diary: *Sorry for the trouble, but it's best that I die. Steve says, I am a waste of space as I have nothing to contribute to this world. Perhaps I might be useful in the next world, wherever that might be.*

Jane was just thirty-five years old.

Epilogue

I am Jane's younger sister.

I wrote the prologue to this book a couple of years ago and put it to one side, but I kept being drawn back to it.

Eventually it became evident to me that I needed to write a book about my family, addiction, and my sister's tragic death.

It is now twenty-five years since Jane took her own life. I was devastated. I felt so guilty (and still do) that I hadn't been a better sister, let her know how much I cared, but I was not in a good place myself, and Jane internalised everything. I had no idea that she was at breaking point.

My father told people that Jane had died of a heart attack, and he even considered leaving her body in Rhodes to be buried. He just couldn't cope and hit the bottle with a vengeance.

It was at my insistence that Jane was repatriated and laid to rest in Northamptonshire. I felt it was the least I could do. I'd failed her in life; I wasn't going to leave her all alone thousands of miles away now that she was dead.

Jane's funeral was stiff and awkward. My father wanted a private service, but I was inundated with phone calls from Jane's friends, who wanted to pay their respects, and so eventually he conceded and allowed a small number of people to attend the church service, but not the burial.

The local newspaper got hold of the story, and 'Suicide on Greek Island' was splashed all over page seven for the entire world to see. My father was furious at the invasion of privacy and, of course, so fearful of being seen as having failed in his role as a parent. He couldn't cope with the shame.

After my sister's tragic death I moved house, threw myself into my music, started performing regularly, and built up a very successful teaching practice. Being busy helped me to cope, and singing is, and always will be, the love of my life and my reason for living.

My father sadly died of his alcohol addiction less than three years after his daughter's death. I bought a beautiful headstone for the family grave. I needed somewhere to go to feel close to my sister, and I hoped that some of her friends would also find visiting her grave a comfort.

Jane has never been far from my thoughts, but following an accident which prevented me from being able to continue with my singing career I have had much more time to reflect on the trauma of losing my sister to suicide. Every time I hear of another young person taking their own life it breaks my heart. We are none of us perfect. There will always be someone better looking, thinner, more talented than us. The pressures of social media and reality TV in this fake world have made people even more insecure and dissatisfied with their lot. People with no talent whatsoever can now become 'famous', and having achieved that, they find that being constantly scrutinised about their appearance or their behaviour has proved too much. Body dysmorphia is extremely common, and still very little is known about the root cause. Recently several of these 'reality stars' have committed suicide. People used to say it was the easy way out, and some religions see it as a sin. Suicide is not so black and white. Those of us that have to continue living never recover from the loss.

I miss my sister desperately and will be forever haunted by how she must have felt in her final hours on this earth to end her life so tragically.

In loving memory of my sister Jane.

I pray you're wrapped in angel's wings protected from the earthly things that led you to such dark despair, to think that no one really cared.